REFORMING
TEACHER EDUCATION
The Impact of the Holmes Group Report

JONAS F. SOLTIS, Editor
Teachers College, Columbia University

D0145224

LIBRARY OF MT. ST. MARY'S COLLEGE EMMITSBURG, MARYLAND

WITHDRAWN

TEACHERS COLLEGE PRESS

Teachers College, Columbia University
New York and London

Published by Teachers College Press, 1234 Amsterdam Avenue, New York, NY 10027

Copyright©1987 by Teachers College, Columbia University

All rights reserved. No part of this publication may be reproduced or transmitted in any form or by any means, electronic or mechanical, including photocopy, or any information storage and retrieval system, without permission from the publisher.

Library of Congress Cataloging-in-Publication Data

Reforming teacher education.

    Includes index.
    1. Tomorrow's teachers. 2. Teachers--Training
of--United States. 3. Universities and colleges--
United States--Curricula--Planning. I. Soltis,
Jonas F.
LB2165.R44 1987   370'.7'10973   87-6427
ISBN 0-8077-2871-3

WITHDRAWN

Manufactured in the United States of America

92 91 90 89 88 87   1 2 3 4 5 6

Contents

Introduction

JONAS F. SOLTIS

Teachers College, Columbia University

One hundred years ago, Teachers College was founded. It soon became acknowledged throughout the world as a leader in the education of teachers. It is fitting, therefore, that the first symposium topic to be addressed during this period of TC's centennial celebration is the reform of teacher education and the continuing development of teaching as a profession. No other social agent outside the family and home can claim to have a greater impact on the intentional shaping of the character and mind of the children and youth in any society than its teachers. They socialize and educate, change and shape lives, instill standards of shared cultural values, create opportunities for individual growth, and provide the knowledge and perspective needed for future citizens to be able to participate effectively in society. There is a fundamental circularity here. The better a teacher is educated, the better an education that teacher potentially can provide. There is also a corollary — the better the teaching environment and the resources provided, the better a teacher's chances of success in helping students obtain a worthwhile and meaningful education. This book is devoted to a discussion of what constitutes a good education for teachers and what sort of teaching environment will provide teachers with the structure and resources they need to be able to meet the high expectations that our society has for education.

Reform of teacher education and the restructuring of the teaching profession are very basic and yet different kinds of educational reform. Past cycles of reform have focused attention primarily on schooling itself, urging such things as changes in the public school curriculum and graduation requirements, raising standards, and motivating teachers by instituting merit pay or career-ladder pay scales. Reform of teacher education and of the teaching profession, on the other hand, means focusing on teaching and taking seriously two assumptions: first, that the best educator is one who is best educated, and second, that the real professional is one who is permitted and encouraged to use expert knowledge and skill autonomously in the intelligent and responsible delivery of high-level services. These two ideas constitute the main themes addressed by the Holmes Group report, *Tomorrow's Teachers*, and by the distinguished contributors to this symposium who were invited to react to the recommendations of the Holmes Group.[1]

This is a historic moment. Not because of the Holmes Group report itself, but because a critical mass seems to be forming with enough force potentially to bring about significant change in America's teaching profession. The public concern with educational reform seems not to be faddish. It has lasted a long time. State governors and legislators, state school officers, local superintendents, business leaders, leaders of teacher organizations and unions, teacher educators themselves, and in the case of the Holmes Group, even the deans of leading schools of education are all thinking and talking seriously about needed long-term reforms in the teaching profession. Thus there is the potential for the balancing of self-interest, reference-group interest, and public interest in a coalition of groups with real power in our nation. No one of them could succeed alone. If they can be brought to see the genuine mutuality of their interests in reforming the teaching profession, and find ways to work together, they just might make history before the century turns.

However, there is also a danger present in this mix. Politicians recognizing the need to compromise may dilute educational ideas with legislative sorts of solutions that lay down restrictive rules and requirements along with the needed money. Business also uses money to get its way and is accustomed to buying the advice of experts, but when acting, may press marketplace solutions rather than sound educational ones. The experts, in this case teachers, administrators, teacher educators, and academics, also have their own problems and shortcomings. Teacher educators exhibit understandable, but nonetheless debilitating, knee-jerk reactions when defending their turf. Academics cannot reach closure; they challenge each other's ideas as a matter of course, and of course there are no unchallengeable positions. Such constant posturing and challenging can be paralyzing. Administrators do have the power to act, but would not want to give up their power over teachers too readily. Teachers have no tradition of playing a major role in the education of young professionals nor of autonomy and choice of their own administrators, nor of peer review. Finally, the public, as holders of the only purse strings we leave them with, are eager for improvement in education but usually not at the expense of increases in state and local taxes.

Nevertheless, if really basic educational and structural reform could be brought about, we would all benefit from a teaching profession made up of bright, able, well-educated persons who have been attracted to teaching as a career of service to youth that encourages initiative and creativity and provides the environment and resources that enable teachers to teach to the best of their ability. This is what makes this book important. It opens up the discussion of the many issues involved in the enterprise of reforming teacher education and advancing the teaching profession.

It is only a beginning, however. After talk and thought, action is required. So is goodwill, goodwill on the part of teachers, teacher unions, administrators, academics, politicians, the business community, and, of course, the

public. We all stand together on the threshold of a potentially historic redec-
laration of our collective democratic belief in the importance of education
and in our respect for those who deliver it. We seek the reform of teaching
in ways to make it a genuine profession, a profession charged with no less
than the shaping of human beings. The stakes are high. We should all enter
and play the game to win — not solely for ourselves nor for our immediate
reference group or constituency, but for all of those yet to become educated
persons and participating members in our democratic society.

Note

1 *Tomorrow's Teachers: A Report of The Holmes Group* (East Lansing, Mich.: The Holmes Group,
1986). Right after the Holmes Group report was made public, the Carnegie Foundation produced
a report dealing with similar matters (*A Nation Prepared: Teachers for the 21st Century*, The Report of
the Carnegie Forum on Education and the Economy's Task Force on Teaching as a Profession
[Washington, D.C.: The Forum, 1986]). A number of the contributors to this symposium have com-
mented on both reports as they treat the reform of the teaching profession.

Tomorrow's Teachers:
The Essential Arguments
of the Holmes Group Report

MICHAEL W. SEDLAK

Michigan State University

This abbreviated version of the Holmes Group report, written by one of the original co-authors of Tomorrow's Teachers, *provides an overview of the proposals for the reform of teacher education that the contributors of this symposium are reacting to.*

The Holmes Group is a consortium of education deans and chief academic officers from the major research universities in each of the fifty states. It was named for Henry W. Holmes, dean of the Harvard Graduate School of Education during the 1920s, who sought to raise the quality and professional status of teacher education. The nucleus of the Holmes Group gathered initially in the autumn of 1983 to consider generally the issues confronting teaching and teacher education. The group has evolved into its present form over the past several years through a series of occasionally painful deliberations on the strengths and weaknesses of teacher education and the profession of teaching in the United States.

   The first public report of the Holmes Group, *Tomorrow's Teachers*, which is the object of this symposium, consists of three related sections: an essay outlining the problems with the status, rewards, and work associated with teaching that jeopardize the recruitment and preparation of qualified teachers; a series of essays introducing and addressing a number of potential obstacles to improving the quality and preparation of the teaching force; and a detailed set of proposals for reform of teaching and teacher education. This article will reconstruct the report's essential arguments for those who have not yet had the opportunity to read the full report. Interested readers are in-

The author would like to express his appreciation to the other authors of Tomorrow's Teachers, *particularly Judith Lanier, David Cohen, Richard Elmore, and Richard Prawat, whose contributions have also been drawn upon in the preparation of this abbreviated version of the Holmes Group Report. It is printed with the permission of the Holmes Group. The author is additionally grateful to Jonas Soltis and Janet Johnson for their insightful recommendations.*

vited to examine the final report's extensive discussions of teaching practice and professional knowledge, central topics of which are only introduced here.

The Holmes Group differs from its predecessors committed to improving the professional preparation of teachers in its recognition that teacher education is largely a creature of teaching itself: its career opportunities, reward structure, traditions of recruitment, working conditions, and authority relations in schools. Without substantial changes in the career of teaching, improvements in the selection and training of teachers will inevitably wither and evaporate. Without addressing the impact of labor-market and working conditions in teaching, schools of education will not be able to attract the clientele they desire, nor will they be able to convince prospective teachers to invest in or endure the sort of extended academic study, professional education, and clinical experience that the Holmes leaders agree is needed. The teaching profession itself must be changed in order to reinforce and protect changes in the level, content, and standards of teacher education. Holmes leaders understand, in other words, that teacher education cannot be reformed significantly without fashioning a market that preferentially rewards graduates of improved programs.

The Holmes Group also differs from most of its predecessors in its appreciation of the necessity of engaging talented teachers and committed administrators in the reform process. The group's leaders are aware of the limited and often unintended results of top-down reform. Just as they recognize that teacher education cannot be improved in isolation, they understand that reforms cannot be arrogantly directed from political offices or academic departments.

These differences in the perspective of the Holmes leadership, coupled with the group's locus in institutions of teacher education, shape the complex, multifront campaign outlined in *Tomorrow's Teachers*. As will become evident from the following discussion of the goals and assumptions presented in the report, the Holmes Group is dedicated not just to the improvement of teacher education but to the construction of a genuine profession of teaching. Briefly, the group's five goals or proposals for action are:

1. To make the education of teachers more intellectually sound; to make prospective teachers thoughtful students of teaching and its improvement. This will require reform of instruction in the preprofessional undergraduate liberal arts and sciences; of subject matter professional pedagogy instruction; and of the clinical experiences in teacher education. Expanding the general education and subject matter exposure of prospective teachers will also require shifting professional academic and clinical studies from the undergraduate to the graduate level.

2. To recognize differences in teachers' knowledge, skill, and commitment, and in their education, certification, work, and career opportunities

by distinguishing among novices, competent professional teachers, and high-level professional leaders. The Holmes Group labels these distinctive practitioners Instructors, Professional Teachers, and Career Professionals. This will require differentiated staffing or role responsibilities in schools as well as differentiated professional education and credentials.

3. To create standards of entry to the profession—examinations and educational requirements—that are professionally relevant and intellectually defensible. This will require imaginative assessments and evaluations.

4. To connect institutions of higher and professional education with schools in order to make better use of expert teachers in the professional education and induction of other teachers and in research on teaching, and to build demonstration sites where new career opportunities, working conditions, and administrative arrangements can be developed and refined. This will require the establishment of new institutional relationships.

5. To make schools better places for teachers to work and for students to learn by altering the professional roles and responsibilities of teachers. This will require changes in the authority relationships in schools and in the nature and scope of autonomy for professional teachers.

Attaining these ambitious goals will obviously depend on the collaboration of individuals associated with a variety of institutions sharing responsibility for shaping the educational enterprise: university academic departments, professional schools of education, school districts, and state houses. In developing these goals and their corollary proposals for action, the Holmes Group anticipated struggles over their implementation and attempted to address many of the most serious concerns that such a broad agenda would inevitably raise in those who will have to change in order to improve our schools and programs of teacher education.

There are far easier ways of getting through the next decade than beginning to implement the Holmes Group proposals. Teacher education programs, for example, could do nothing and get rich as the demand for teachers swells their enrollments. Many faculty members in the academic departments would probably prefer to be left alone to allow the reward structures of their disciplines to shape what is allowed to pass as undergraduate education. The Holmes Group leaders recognize, however, that demographic and social trends have conspired to leave us faced in the next decade with the task of staffing classrooms with the teachers who will remain in schools well into the twenty-first century. To allow this opportunity—which might not return for forty years—to slip away would be foolish and destructive.

CAREERS

The traditions of recruitment, norms of preparation, and conditions of work in schools have severely hindered efforts to improve the quality of teaching. This unfortunate legacy was created by the youthful, transient, and large work forced needed to staff our schools as the United States attempted to achieve universal education. During the perennial shortages that have plagued teaching during the past century or more, the nation relied on the generous subsidy of those whose opportunities were limited by prejudice and civic customs in employment, particularly women and minorities. Shortages were handled with emergency certificates and inordinately weak credentials. Such deceptive remedies created the illusion that all was well by masking the crucial distinction between covering classes and providing effective teaching. These norms and traditions contributed to a flat career pattern, roundly condemned as teaching's "careerlessness," where ambition and accomplishment went unrewarded both in terms of expanded responsibilities and autonomy, and higher salaries.

The Holmes Group recognizes that teaching's traditional career structure, increasingly dysfunctional in the face of changed social and demographic realities, must be changed if the quality of teaching and teacher education is to be improved. Employment options for women and minorities have expanded dramatically over the past twenty years. Coupled with increasing stress on the job and a decline in real purchasing power, such opportunities accelerated the defection of competent teachers from the profession and discouraged many promising prospective teachers from ever entering it. The imminent shortage of qualified teachers makes our response to the problems of recruitment, preparation, induction, and retention more critical than at any point in our nation's history. For the first time, the desirability of a teaching career will be tested in an open labor market. If we respond as we have in the past by relying on emergency certificates and spurious credentials, unprecedented numbers of incompetent teachers will be hired. Circumstances will keep them in the classroom. Their abilities and posture toward professional responsibility will shape the norms and effects of teaching for years to come.

Based on this understanding of the problems associated with the prevailing career structure in teaching, the Holmes Group endorses the concept of differentiated staffing in order to improve the quality, engagement, and commitment of the teaching force. To attract, prepare, and retain a truly competent teaching force, intellectually capable adults must have more flexible access to the classroom. We must counteract the confining role definition for teachers that discourages many effective practitioners from remaining in their classrooms. Improving teaching's attraction and retention powers requires a differentiated professional teaching force able to respond to the opportunities provided by a staged career that would make and reward formal distinctions about responsibilities and degrees of autonomy.

Differentiating the teaching career would be advantageous to individuals, public schools, and professional schools of education. It would make it possible for districts to go beyond limited financial incentives and to challenge and reward commitment. This is essential to encourage teachers to reinvest in their work, and earn rewards while remaining in their classrooms; it would also counterbalance the defection of talented, committed teachers into administration. Some occupational mobility and choice, so absent today, would help to ease the frustrations that drive talented teachers from their classrooms.

Differentiated staffing would make it possible for communities to respond to disequilibrium in the supply of and demand for teachers. Instead of lowering standards and awarding full professional status to individuals with questionable preparation, differentiated staffing would permit responsible expansion and contraction of a pool of teachers, while protecting the integrity of the teaching force. A hierarchy of levels of responsibility corresponding to degrees of professional education, experience, and performance evaluations would make it possible to adjust to spot shortages in specific fields, or to more generalized shortages, by adding, subtracting, or shifting personnel resources in a fashion far more rational than is customary today. It would be possible to limit the autonomy of certain teachers who would work under supervision, thereby avoiding the traditional practice of bestowing full professional prerogatives on everyone brought into the classroom, regardless of their credentials or demonstrated abilities.

Finally, since the Holmes Group understands the reciprocity between teaching and teacher education, differentiating the career would enhance professional schools of education. Expanding career opportunities and rewards in teaching would create a market for professionally trained teachers with advanced graduate credentials.

A differentiated profession would be built on the distinctive contributions of three groups of practitioners. The first group, which the Holmes Group calls *Instructors*, would be bright, well-educated adults interested in teaching a specific subject without making a career commitment to teaching. They might be undecided about a vocation, or prefer to teach children as secondary work. Because of their limited exposure to professional knowledge, Instructors would have their lessons structured and supervised. They would not set school policy, determine curricula, or evaluate personnel or programs. They would possess limited rights, responsibilities, and benefits. They would not have tenure, nor autonomy and the obligations afforded fully professional teachers. The Instructors' contribution to education, despite their limited investment in a teaching career, would be invaluable to the schools.

Obviously the teaching force should not consist entirely of individuals who participate on a temporary or limited basis. Capable college graduates must also be encouraged to invest fully in a teaching career. Such *Professional Teachers*, constituting the profession's backbone, deserve working conditions that support sustained success, and they need alternatives in schools to accommodate their different aspirations. Unlike Instructors, Professional Teachers would be certified as fully autonomous practitioners, entitled to exercise their classroom duties without supervision. They would be specialists in both subject matter and pedagogy. They would understand the core ideas in the subjects they teach, the probable learning problems children encounter at different ages, and the multiple ways by which teachers can overcome these problems. They would not only be effective instructors, but would also be better prepared to function as child advocates to ensure that schools and communities served, in the broadest sense, the educational needs of their children. Many teachers thrive on this intensely focused role in school. They find their success in instruction rewarding, and their training, creativity, and commitment are best directed toward their classrooms. Nothing should undermine their effective instruction in the subjects and grade levels for which they have demonstrated competence.

Other teachers, however, would appreciate and benefit from alternatives to their work directly with children. Interested more broadly in educational policy and improvement, they would like to collaborate with other adults on problems related to school effectiveness. Providing opportunities for these *Career Professionals* would improve the educational effectiveness of other adults in schools. Presumably they would participate in teacher education (guiding Instructors, for example, or providing staff development opportunities), curriculum improvement, and testing and measurement, or conduct action research. Although they would constitute perhaps 20 percent of a school's staff, Career Professionals would play a key role in revitalizing the teaching profession.

Some occupations have used differentiated staffing to make artificial and counterproductive distinctions in the workplace, to fabricate hierarchies in order to claim higher status and autonomy. Holmes Group leaders are aware of such problems and caution against their replication in teaching. Large, complex organizations, nevertheless, do become hierarchical: Educational institutions have been so for more than a century. The problem lies not with differentiation and hierarchy, but with illegitimate, irrational, and spurious distinctions. Rational, differentiated staffing based on defensible differences in training, authority, and responsibilities will make it possible to respond fairly to the complexities of teaching and learning in large, diverse institutions. The question is not whether hierarchies will persist in educational organizations. The question is whether they will be based on defensible, rational distinctions, or on the flight from teaching and traditions of sexism, as they ordinarily are in schools today.

TEACHING

To change the preparation of teachers and the nature of instructional work in schools, the Holmes Group recognizes that it is essential to challenge prevailing views of teaching that oversimplify the knowledge, skills, and dispositions essential to effective and equitable practice. Many people, for example, hold an inaccurate, excessively simple "bright-person" model of teaching. They have been convinced that teaching is a one-way process of delivery, of crafting a lesson and presenting it to a group of prospective learners. In their view, the onus of learning rests entirely on the students. To them the characteristics of the classroom group, and the individuals in it, influence the lesson and mode of delivery only modestly. The teachers' responsibility basically ends when they have told students what they must remember to know and do. If effective teaching actually consisted of such behavior, most individuals who knew something of a subject could easily teach it. But this view blithely overlooks critical aspects of quality teaching—particularly the extent to which lessons are appropriate only for the specific students for whom a teacher is responsible and for whom the lesson should be crafted.

Unfortunately, simple and naive models of teaching are often most attractive to bright, studious individuals who took major responsibility for their own learning as students. Reasoning that what worked for them will work for others, they believe that everyone else can just as easily survive a teacher intent on just presenting the material. Such a belief can too easily ignore or disparage professional knowledge because it assumes that teachers' lessons can have quality independent of student learning.

The Holmes Group challenges such naive linear definitions of teaching. It offers in contrast a vision of teaching and learning that is fundamentally interactive. The professional knowledge that competent teachers possess goes beyond a strong, coherent liberal education. It is not merely common sense, nor is it learned only through trial-and-error teaching or the experience of being a student. Rather, it includes academic and clinical learning that prepares one to manage both mastery of content and the complex social relations of the classroom in a way that fosters student learning as well as an attachment to learning. Because of this shared interactive view of the learning process, Holmes leaders are convinced that the knowledge, skills, and dispositions essential to effective teaching are acquired through extended professional education.

LIBERAL EDUCATION

Aggravating the problems of the bright-person model is the reality of learning in the arts and sciences at the undergraduate level. Improving the education of any prospective teacher is impossible without the concomitant reform of the nonprofessional components of the undergraduate curriculum. Students pursuing their professional studies must arrive already equipped with a sound command of the undergirding disciplines and have developed the qualitites of engaged, inquiring learners. As a number of scathing reports have recently demonstrated, it is difficult for undergraduates, regardless of whether they intend to teach, to develop such skills. The prevailing pattern of fragmented, excessively specialized, and prematurely vocationalized curricula, coupled with uninspired pedagogy, does not provide appropriate models of intellectual coherency and engagement.

At best, the contemporary academic major is largely a preparation for graduate study in a disciplinary field. This limited vision and focus often fails to elaborate the structure of the discipline, its origins and goals, and ignores criteria that would allow learners to distinguish between issues meriting deep study and other more trivial topics. Traditional baccalaureate study fails teachers who, at all levels, must find and present the most powerful and generative ideas in a way that both preserves the integrity of disciplinary knowledge and leads students to understand a subject. It is too easy for critics of teacher education to say that prospective teachers need simply to take more courses in the arts and sciences. The disarray of knowledge in the disciplines has been well documented.

Holmes Group leaders understand how hard it is to change the curricula and pedagogy of the disciplines, and how costly it is to confront the prevailing reward structures of most academic departments. Improving the quality of teaching, nevertheless, depends on changing the course selection patterns, class content, and existing pedagogy encountered by prospective teachers during their preprofessional studies. Such reform would not only benefit prospective teachers, however, but would strengthen the higher education of all college students.

PROFESSIONAL EDUCATION

Reforming the education of teachers depends on engaging in the complex work of identifying the knowledge base for competent teaching, and developing the content and strategies whereby it can be effectively mastered. Although specialized professional knowledge has been under development for some time — and dramatic strides have been made during the past two decades — an amalgam of intuition, unreflective reactions, and personal dispositions still seems to ground the right to teach.

Basically a "nonprogram" at present, professional studies are rarely interrelated or coherent. The curriculum is seldom reviewed for its comprehensiveness, its redundancy, or its responsiveness to research and analysis. Advisement is too often ineffective, leaving students to wander about rather than progressing systematically in a cohort through their programs.

Building on an increasingly mature body of scholarship and empirical research, a program of professional studies in education must integrate at least five components to qualify as a comprehensive plan for teacher preparation. The first is the study of teaching and schooling as an academic field. This would provide a description and explanation of the phenomenon of schooling itself — its development, its purpose, and the macro and micro mechanisms that make schooling possible and sustain it. The second is knowledge of the pedagogy of subject matter. This would consist of the ability to reformulate content knowledge so as to engage a variety of pupils and to strengthen the critical acumen necessary to judge the value of available curricula for particular settings and goals. Such pedagogical expertise is essential to bridge personal understanding and the capacity to teach. A related third component is comprised of the skills and understandings implicit in classroom teaching — creating a communal setting where students of varying ability have the opportunity to develop and learn. Building such an environment requires values, dispositions, and a sense of ethical responsibility: the fourth component of a comprehensive program of professional education for teaching.

The academic pedagogical studies common to most colleges of education routinely fail to develop such essential professional knowledge, skills, and dispositions in the teachers they prepare. As it is customarily encountered, the clinical, or fifth, component of the pedagogical studies program similarly fails to strengthen the professional qualities needed to ensure effective classroom instruction. Virtually every evaluator of teacher education concludes that program graduates attribute their success to their student teaching and early induction experiences. Many reformers recommend that the entire teacher education program be infused with such clinical opportunities.

The Holmes Group, however, is skeptical about widely held claims for the benefits of the traditional clinical experience. Although students value it most highly, as do their counterparts in all professional preparation programs, the prospective teacher's field experience is neither broad nor deep. Cooperating teachers are usually arbitrarily assigned and too often lack essential professional knowledge and skills needed to strengthen the learning of prospective teachers. University supervision is infrequent. It is common for the experience to be limited to a single school, classroom, and teacher, and it rarely builds on the general principles and theories emphasized in earlier university study. Everyone does well. Yet most students quickly conform to the expectations and practices of their single supervising teacher, and rarely put novel techniques into practice or risk failure. They succeed so easily because they relinquish the norms of professional colleges of education without a struggle. The experience emphasizes imitation of and subservience to the supervising teacher, not investigation, reflection, and problem solving.

Holmes Group leaders believe that university faculty and selected clinical staff from cooperating schools need to reexamine contemporary professional pedagogical offerings to produce an articulate, coherent curriculum with intellectual integrity. Similarly, they endorse clinical experiences in multiple sites with youngsters of diverse ability, motivation, and cultural background.

PROFESSIONAL DEVELOPMENT SCHOOLS

Recognizing the interdependence of teaching and teacher education suggests a promising alternative to traditional sites for preparing teachers. Professional development schools, the analogue to medical education's teaching hospitals, would bring practicing teachers and administrators together with university faculty in partnerships that improve teaching and learning on the part of their respective students. Such schools would largely overcome many of the problems with traditional academic clinical and pedagogical studies by providing opportunities for teachers and administrators to influence the development of their profession, and for university faculty to increase the professional relevance of their work. These institutions assume that improving teaching ultimately depends on providing teachers with opportunities to contribute to the development of professional knowledge and practice, to form collegial relationships beyond their immediate working environment, and to mature intellectually as they expand the range of their responsibilities. Such collaborative sites would help university-based research and instruction to strengthen its professional roots in practice and to maintain the professional schools' vitality and credibility.

In addition to improving teacher education, professional development schools would expand opportunities for strengthening knowledge and practice: to test different instructional arrangements under different working and administrative conditions. Innovative professional practice would be developed, demonstrated, and critically evaluated at these exemplary sites before being disseminated elsewhere.

Finally, professional development schools would strengthen the profession by serving as models of promising and productive structural relations among Instructors, Professional Teachers, Career Professionals, and administrators. Improving these relations, expanding opportunities and responsibilities, would make working conditions attractive enough to entice talented novices and to retain dedicated, competent teachers. Such a program would provide an optimally balanced plan of study and experience for the neophyte under the tutelage of teacher educators and teachers working in the vanguard of practice. It would offer talented teachers who love their work and want to improve it a means of advancing without leaving the classroom, physically or psychologically.

CREDENTIALS

Recommending that the status of teaching be elevated by raising standards, improving career opportunities through differentiated staffing, and reforming both professional education and instruction in the liberal arts and sciences has its potential pitfalls. Because the undertaking would be costly to individuals and institutions alike, it is essential to anticipate and overcome the unintended, undesirable consequences of such ambitious proposals. Earlier initiatives in education and other occupations, shaped by similar dedication to tougher standards and professionalism, have shown that good intentions alone cannot prevent several predictable problems. New credentials themselves, for example, are easily abused. Individuals unfamiliar with the examination and certification processes, most commonly minorities, are too often excluded. By misrepresenting what practitioners can actually do, credentialing can ultimately erode the public's trust in the quality of a profession. Problems with credentials can lead individuals to squander money, time, and energy, and can cause institutions to waste resources. Even worse, problems with the integrity of credentials can lead to outright quackery: providing services that actually harm clients.

Schools have a special relation to the public. Because education is compulsory for all citizens, teaching and teacher education have a unique obligation to avoid the pitfalls of credentialism. Education must resist the temptation to enrich itself as other occupations have done, by offering mediocre performance behind a facade of higher credentials. We cannot pretend that raising credential standards for teachers is the same as improving teaching.

Teaching can improve its professional status only by improving its effectiveness — by raising the level of children's achievement and deepening their engagement with learning. Similarly, teacher education's professional status can be improved only by bestowing genuine credentials that reflect the highest standards and the most rigorous preparation possible.

There are several forms of irresponsible credentialism of which teaching and teacher education must be particularly aware, particularly the trap of *pseudo-credentialism*: bestowing credentials regardless of demonstrated ability. Pseudo-credentialism does not require professional schools to raise their standards or to improve the quality of the education they offer. It allows them to continue what they have been doing by awarding a different credential. Pseudo-credentialism takes different forms in different occupations. Teachers, for example, are paid according to the number of credits earned beyond the bachelor's degree, regardless of whether additional graduate education improved their teaching. State-imposed continuing certification requirements routinely benefit teachers and teacher educators financially, with little regard to the substance or rigor of the advanced credentials invested in or awarded. Teacher educators must not simply add on course requirements, endorse standardized examinations, or demand a fifth year of training without rethinking the value of such changes. Regardless of the form that it takes, pseudo-credentialism is a powerful weapon in the arsenal of opportunistic professionalization and must be challenged.

The potential abuse of credentials, however, should not lead us to reject professional education and certification, and to replace them with the assumption that those who know something can automatically teach. Opening the entitlement to teach to the open market — one response to the disenchantment with the abuse of existing credentials — would not solve the problem of teacher quality. Indeed, as noted above, *deregulation*, as this strategy is called, would aggravate the learning difficulties of many children.

The Holmes Group recognizes that rejecting professional education in favor of allowing college graduates from the academic disciplines to assume full responsibility for classroom instruction only substitutes one form of pseudo-credentialism for another. In one case the credential consists of doing whatever is necessary to complete a traditional teacher education program (ordinarily maintaining a minimum grade-point average and passing specified courses in order to accumulate credits). In the other case, the credential consists of doing whatever is necessary to earn a bachelor's degree in one of the disciplines (by similarly accumulating course credits and maintaining a specified grade-point average). Course grades and the accumulation of credits constitute the coinage of both credentials. In neither case is real teaching ability being required, recognized, or developed. Neither case necessarily produces good teachers. Neither approach is likely to help us respond effectively to the situation we face.

Just as there is a role for higher education to play in building maturity and disciplinary knowledge, there is a role for professional education to play in strengthening prospective teachers' understanding of responsibility, developing their ability to engage students, and cooperatively guiding their induction into the classroom. The Holmes Group proposes an alternative of legitimate professional education and certification to the forms of irresponsible credentialism outlined above. Endorsing professional education does not imply that real performance evaluations will not be made, or that the credentials will be accepted in lieu of on-the-job assessments of teaching ability. The issue is how to prepare the pool of teachers who are to be allowed to be evaluated. The problem is how to prepare the pool of teachers who will earn the highest assessments for their instructional effectiveness.

CONCLUSION

Struggling to address these potential obstacles to improving teaching and teacher education, and anticipating and answering the vital questions that they raise, has strengthened the Holmes Group leaders' understanding of the reform process and their appreciation of the opportunities that will open over the ensuing decade. As the Holmes agenda is implemented, there will inevitably be many mistakes, false starts, and unanticipated problems. Solutions that work in one setting may require adaptation to work in another. Because the group recognizes the necessity of adaptation as the strengths and weaknesses of its vision and proposals are exposed, Holmes leaders are committed to responding imaginatively with a variety of alternatives and to sharing the wisdom of experience with all Holmes institutions and with the other individuals and organizations whose cooperation is essential to improving teaching and teacher education in the United States.

Teaching: International Concerns

PHILIP G. ALTBACH
State University of New York, Buffalo

Offering a comparative perspective, Altbach looks at the prestige accorded European secondary school teachers, the undereducated third world teaching force, the seeming lack of relation between teacher education and different levels of international achievement, and current teacher reforms in Japan and Russia.

Tomorrow's Teachers reflects American concerns and issues of policy relating to the United States. However, some of the broader issues reflected in the Holmes Group report, and also in the more recent Report of the Carnegie Forum on Education and the Economy's Task Force on Teaching as a Profession, *A Nation Prepared: Teachers for the 21st Century*, have significant international relevance. An international perspective can add to the debate on the future of the teaching profession in America. Too often, we tend to think only about our own situation — Americans are especially guilty of insularity in this respect. Yet the experiences of other countries can be useful in framing issues and raising questions. While it is seldom possible to copy innovations and practices from overseas, a comparative perspective can be a valuable exercise in consciousness-raising.

Concern about the teaching profession is worldwide. Many countries have realized that teachers are at the center of the educational process and that without good teachers, all other innovations are doomed to failure. While other educational reforms, such as educational technology and satellite-based delivery systems, remain important, teachers have again become a major concern of planners in many countries. There is also widespread dissatisfaction with the current situation of schooling in many nations — and teachers have come in for their share of criticism.

In the Third World, there is concern that a sufficient number of teachers be provided and that these teachers have appropriate training. Virtually no one advocates providing teachers with education in their subject specialties alone — all stress the importance of a distinctive training specifically for teaching. Agencies like the World Bank have spent large amounts of money on the improvement of teacher training. Significantly, few argue now that formal schooling is a bad thing and that people should be liberated through education by nonformal means. The ideas of Ivan Illich and Paulo Freire, so popular a few years ago, have much less influence today. Where they remain powerful, the stress is on "humanizing" traditional schools. For the Third World, schools have become important. Planners worry that poor countries have neither the financial nor the personnel resources to ensure an adequate supply of well-trained teachers, and some have stressed other means of ensuring a minimal standard of educational quality. For example, the provision of textbooks of a high standard and in sufficient numbers has been seen as a way of reinforcing the quality of education in a situation where teachers may be poorly trained.

Some argue that the cost of education in the Third World is too high and there are efforts to find ways of providing schooling at lower cost. While there is a recognition that teacher quality is often low — in many countries, primary teachers in rural areas have less than a secondary school education — upgrading teaching and ensuring a higher standard of quality is a very difficult problem. Planners turn to private initiative as a means of reducing governmental expenditures, to improved textbooks, and in a few instances to the use of technology. Few now argue that massive funding should be provided to upgrade the teaching profession in the Third World. World Bank efforts to improve teacher training facilities, however, are evident in a number of countries. While it is an oversimplification to claim that teachers are not part of the blueprint for educational improvement in the Third World, it is certainly true that there is considerable confusion about priorities and an implicit belief that significantly upgrading the teaching profession may be too difficult.

In many countries the gulf between primary and secondary schools is much greater than it is in the United States. In Europe, until recently, secondary schooling was not universal. The academic stream of the secondary system, limited to a minority, was seen as elitist and prestigious. Teachers in these academic secondary schools had high prestige and relatively high salaries, and were graduates of the best universities. They had little, if any, training in the field of education. In much of Europe, secondary school teachers, even in the vocational streams, have considerably higher prestige and salaries than their compeers in primary schools. They have considerably more professional autonomy as well. In some countries, primary and secondary teachers belong to different professional organizations or unions. The trend in Europe toward American-style comprehensive schooling has not broken the distinction between primary and secondary education.

It is at least possible that the lack of distinct differentiation between primary and secondary teaching in terms of teacher preparation, working conditions, and prestige in the United States may cause some problems in terms of creating a professional cadre of secondary school teachers. If secondary school teachers had the self-image and status of European teachers, it might be easier to introduce the kinds of reform proposed by the Holmes Group. Indeed, it might well be worth examining carefully the pattern of professionalization of teacher education and the working conditions of secondary school teachers in Western Europe.

If the Holmes Group proposals help to create a differentiated professional cadre of teachers in the United States, the American teaching profession may move in a European direction of different levels of prestige and remuneration, and as a result the common identity of the profession might be diminished. This is not necessarily a negative development, but it is one worth considering as patterns of teacher preparation and the articulation between training and professional work in schools are altered. The logic of the Holmes Group proposals seems increasingly to differentiate between primary and secondary teacher preparation and in this respect the Western European experience may be quite relevant.

One might well question the correlation between the quality of teacher preparation or even the innate ability of the teachers and student achievement. Because the international studies of educational achievement have not factored teacher quality or teacher preparation into their explanations of differences in student achievement in different countries, the correlation between teacher preparation and student achievement in school is not very clear. Countries with high academic achievement do not necessarily have impressive programs of teacher preparation. It is perhaps significant that few look toward Japanese teacher preparation programs as a model for other countries despite the fact that Japan has a high level of academic achievement in the international comparisons.

There is concern about the quality and funding of education in many countries. Teacher education is part of plans for reform in most of the plans for change. In the Soviet Union a major blueprint for educational reform is now being implemented that will have far-reaching implications for the educational system. The basic thrust is to vocationalize the curriculum and make education more relevant to Soviet technological development. But teacher education is a part of the overall reform. India has also promulgated a national reform plan, aimed at decreasing the weight of educational credentialism (a heritage of British colonialism) and vocationalizing secondary and higher education. Teachers are not a major focus of this effort. The Japanese are talking about "humanizing" their highly effective school system. Many worry about the intense pressure of the examination system, the high rate of teenage suicide, and the tendency of Japanese students to memorize lessons rather than evaluate what they learn. In a sense, the Japanese are moving toward an American approach to education just as the United States is adopting more of the competitive orientation of the Japanese. Teachers play a key role in Japanese educational thinking, since it is the classroom environment that is basic to a redirection of the philosophy of education.

What does this tell us about current efforts in the United States to reform teacher education, and particularly about the Holmes Group's proposals? For one thing, the process of educational reform at any level and in any country is a difficult process. The rate of success is not impressive. Even in highly centralized nations, such as the Soviet Union, China, or Japan, educational reforms are difficult to implement and they frequently have unintended consequences. Typically, reforms are stimulated by a perceived crisis and proposed by authorities at the top. However, since implementation must take place at the bottom, it is frequently difficult to ensure that policies are put into practice. The Holmes Group has one advantage in that its proposals have emerged from those actually involved in the process of teacher education. The commitment to implementation comes from those who developed the plans. The Holmes proposals also dovetail with national concerns for the improvement of secondary education in America, and the congruence of national concern with local planning may yield some interesting results. A disadvantage of the Holmes Group, of course, is the fact that the reformers represent only a small segment of the teacher training community in the United States, and there are many interests, philosophies, and orientations at stake.

A universal problem of educational reform is that of funding. While some of the Holmes Group proposals can be implemented by teacher training institutions without a massive outlay of funds, full implementation will require considerable money as well as a significant restructuring of the teaching profession and the involvement of education decision makers at many levels. It will be extremely difficult to ensure that the efforts of both funding agencies and decision makers are coordinated. The experience of other countries is that without a massive push from the top or a major crisis, the implementation of complex educational reforms is quite difficult. What some Japanese observers have called the "big bang" theory of educational reform is needed. It is not clear that teachers, policymakers, or the public see the current state of the American teaching profession as one of crisis at the present time.

Education is in crisis in a number of countries and significant reforms have been proposed and are being implemented. In a few, the teaching profession is perceived as a major component of the reform. Overall, however, it is the case that American reforms have recently paid more attention to the teaching profession than has been the case overseas. If one looks abroad for effective models of educational change, one will be frustrated, since the process of reform is a difficult one regardless of the structure of society or the patterns of education. A look abroad can provide some insights into worldwide educational concerns and patterns of change. In some respects, the Holmes Group is charting new territory in educational reform, not only in the content of the proposals but also in terms of the process of developing the plans.

Will the Social Context Allow a Tomorrow for *Tomorrow's Teachers?*

MICHAEL W. APPLE
University of Wisconsin, Madison

First asking why schools and teachers should be called on to solve social and economically created structural problems in our society, Apple then raises related economic questions about how minorities and working-class students will pay for additional professional education and whether communities intent on keeping taxes low will maintain a lopsided temporary teacher workforce. He also warns of taking a scientific-technical view of teacher education.

There is a good deal to applaud in *Tomorrow's Teachers*. The report is quite insightful in a number of areas. For instance, in opposition to the very reductive proposals now surfacing in the media and elsewhere that blame the school for all of our social ills, the authors at least minimally recognize how closely tied the educational system is to social factors outside its doors. "Excellence" and responsiveness in schooling may require profound alterations in the unequal economic and political relations that dominate the larger society.

Second, the report shows its willingness to deal with complexity in its assertion (one that I believe is very well founded) that teaching is not reducible to "competencies" measured on paper-and-pencil tests. Rather, good teaching is a complex assemblage of knowledge "that," "how," and "to," none of which can be easily merged back into the others. Third, the authors' recognition of the gendered specificities out of which many of the conditions of teaching were constructed is commendable. It is the case that whatever excellence our school system now has was built on the backs of the low-paid and committed labor of generations of teachers who were primarily women.[1] No other report of this type has dealt honestly with this critically important issue. I do not believe that the Holmes Group goes far enough with this recognition, but it is to the authors' credit that the question of *who* does the bulk of the teaching in the United States is at least raised. Any call for greater control over the teaching profession, any attempt to change teachers' work, is also a call to control the labor process of what is largely "women's work" and needs to be seen in the context of the frequent attempts to rationalize women's paid work in the past.[2]

Fourth, the wish to involve schools and especially teachers more directly in teacher education, to form more cooperative arrangements, is a clear sign of progress. It values the practical and political skills teachers have developed over decades of hard work. Further, and very importantly, such involvement could assist in the movement to resist the deskilling of teaching that has accelerated in the past few years.[3] The same could be said of the group's position on the necessity of more cooperative relations between faculties of education and the rest of the university.

Finally, *Tomorrow's Teachers* is clear about many of the dangers of short-term solutions to the problems confronting teaching. It rightly raises cautions about credential deregulation, a process that could have the same truly negative effects as other privatized and deregulated proposals such as voucher plans.[4] And it is self-reflective about some of the dangers of simple models of differentiated staffing. All of these points document why we should take the Holmes Group's recommendations seriously. Even though I have disagreements with a number of their specific proposals, the thoughtfulness and care that went into crafting their position is evident.

Even with the articulateness of these proposals, there are gaps and silences in the document. What I want to do here is raise a series of issues that need to be given further consideration. Obviously, these will by nature take the form of assertions that cannot be detailed in depth given space limitations. Interested readers who wish to pursue these claims will find further substantiation in the references that accompany these comments. I shall limit my attention to a few issues that may not usually surface in discussions of the document.

A number of points need to be made at the outset. The supposed crisis in teaching and in education in general is not an isolated phenomenon. It is related to a much more extensive structural crisis in the economy, in ideology, and in authority relations. As I have argued in considerably more detail elsewhere, we are witnessing an attempt to restructure nearly all of our major cultural, economic, and political institutions to bring them more closely into line with the needs of only a very limited segment of the American population.[5] Thus, we cannot fully understand why our formal institutions of education and the teachers and administrators who work so long and hard in them are being focused on so intently today unless we realize that economically powerful groups and the New Right have already been partly successful in refocusing attention away from the very real problems of inequality in the economy and in political representation and shifting most criticism to the health, welfare, legal, and especially educational systems. In technical terms, there has been a marked shift from a concern for "person rights" to those of "property rights" in our public discourse.[6]

In essence, dominant groups have been relatively successful in *exporting* the larger crisis away from themselves. When achievement is low among certain groups, when there are significant rates of negative intergenerational mobility, when workers have little enthusiasm for their jobs, and so forth, the public is asked to blame the school and the teachers. That is, rather than focusing directly on what may be the major sources of the problem — for instance, the immensely high under- and unemployment rates among working-class and especially minority youth who often see little future for themselves, an economy in which 80 percent of the benefits consistently go to the top 20 percent of the population, corporate decisions that cause millions of employees to work in low-paid, deskilled, and boring jobs (or to have no jobs at all), or an economic system that by its very nature needs to subvert traditional values, authority relations, self-discipline, and accepted conceptions of legitimate knowledge in order to create new "needs" and to stimulate the purchasing of commodities, and so forth[7] — the problem is placed on the educational system. If only teachers were better prepared, if only teaching and curricula were more tightly controlled and better managed, if only textbooks were more demanding and discipline and work skills were stressed, all of the above problems would be solved. The diagnosis and cure are actually a form of category error and would be easy to dismiss on empirical grounds if only they were not taken so seriously.

Tomorrow's Teachers, then, needs to be seen as something that follows in the footsteps of other documents such as *A Nation at Risk*. Its authors are considerably more aware of the larger structural situation in which schools and teachers exist and they are certainly not apologists for those people who wish to turn schools over to industrial and conservative needs and ideologies. The existing process of exporting the blame and bringing conservative ideologies into the heart of the educational enterprise helps, however, to construct the context in which the report of the Holmes Group will be *read* even though this may not be the authors' intention at all.

Obviously, *Tomorrow's Teachers* cannot solve all of these larger problems. No document about teachers and teaching could. But it is wise to keep the structural context in mind, since — while educators should direct their attention to what needs to be done in education — education itself must be wary of assuming that the answers to many of its very real dilemmas lie in preparing a more intellectually rigorous "profession." To do this may simply play into the hands of the attempt by dominant groups to export their crisis onto other areas. Thus, while I am in total agreement with the Holmes Group that some important things must be done in education and in teacher education, the latent effects of limiting our attention to the internal issues need to be given a good deal of thought.

While I want to avoid being overly economistic here, let me use this larger social context as a backdrop to point to some of the economic problems that I believe will create serious difficulties in the way the report of the Holmes

Group will be received. It may produce effects that its authors would not intend or approve.

There is one serious problem that needs to be given considerably more attention by those institutions and individuals that wish to take the report's recommendations seriously. Here I am speaking of the class and racial dynamics that could evolve in the elimination of an undergraduate education major. The Holmes report partly recognizes the fact that extending teacher training beyond the fourth year could present problems for some individuals. Hence, it calls for loan forgiveness for future teachers. Yet the problems go much deeper than this. Already, large numbers of students must work one and sometimes two jobs to make enough money to live on and pay college expenses during their four years of college. We are witnessing a severe downturn in minority and working-class college enrollments. Many universities have become bastions of the middle class and above. Extending professional training beyond the four years will simply have elitist effects unless large sums of money are made available not just in "forgiveable" tuition loans but in outright grants for living expenses, books, and so on. Absent this much more extensive financial commitment, the outcome of the Holmes Group recommendations will be to ultimately make it more difficult for less economically advantaged individuals to become teachers. Without such extensive financial support, movements to increase the amount of time spent in teacher education should be resisted, since their class- and race-stratifying effects could be massive.

The economic issues do not end here, however. Other elements of the report need further thought as well. The plan to have differentiated staffing patterns, for example, has major economic implications that may be hidden beneath the meritorious goals of the Holmes Group. In arguing for changes in the constitution of teaching we must realize that we live in the real world, a world of declining revenues, of anger over school budgets, of pressure to cut educational costs as much as possible. I do not like this situation, but it will not go away. These conditions — caused in large part by the fiscal crisis of the state[8] — are already creating immense pressures on local school districts to hire the least expensive teachers possible. With differentiated staffing, I would predict that many school systems will attempt to minimize costs by hiring as many Instructors as possible. These short-term, nontenured appointments would save districts a good deal of money. Pension costs would be minimal. There would be a continual large turnover of staff, even more than today. Thus, the bulk of the teaching force would be made up of those people have less than five years seniority. The salary savings here would be enormous. The fiction of a reprofessionalized teaching force might be maintained, but there would be considerable pressure to minimize the number of Professional Teachers and to keep to a bare minimum the number of

Career Professionals. The fiscal crisis is not a fiction, as anyone who works with school budgets knows. Any plan to differentiate teaching that does not include serious proposals to deal with the possible management offensive to cut costs that will undoubtedly arise from such plans is not as complete as it should be.

These economic points have important implications. The Holmes Group, as a group made up primarily of deans of major research institutions, needs to engage in intense and concerted lobbying and to put pressure on state legislatures and the federal government not only in support of its proposals, but just as importantly for considerable sums of money for students in these extended programs to live on. This can be accomplished only if organizations such as the Holmes Group join with others in questioning where financial resources are now going (i.e., into "defense," corporate tax "relief," etc.). Absent such alterations in our current "income transfer policies" (in which funding for human programs is transferred, say, to the military), the resources available to actually make a long-term difference will probably be insufficient. This may be hard for educators like ourselves to deal with, but we need to face up to how very complicated and far reaching the dilemmas we face actually are and what may actually be required to solve them.

Furthermore, guarantees need to be given by every school district that accepts models of differentiated staffing and career ladders similar to those proposed by the Holmes Group about the hiring ratios. This too will require money for financially crisis-ridden communities and will again require a significant reorientation of spending priorities at all levels, but especially at the national level. There are plans available for such changes both in spending priorities and in social goals, some of which are insightful and detailed. These take the common good, not only the needs of business, industry, and the Right, as their starting point, and integrate educational planning into proposals for more democratic planning in general.[9] These plans provide a platform on which we can stand and from which we can see the role of education in its larger context. I am afraid that without movement toward these kinds of more general changes, reports like that of the Holmes Group may play into the hands of the conservative restoration.

Let me raise one final caution. In a document produced by representatives of many of the major research institutions in education, it is not surprising that a faith in "science" as the primary road to pedagogic and curricular "progress" should be evident. I must admit, however, to having some serious reservations about the claim in *Tomorrow's Teachers* that the "promise of science of education is about to be fulfilled" (p. 52). The very metaphor of a science of education is problematic. Education may not in fact "progress" in quite the same manner as even the most applied of the sciences.[10]

If by science we mean the more historical European idea of disciplined reason enlivened by a concern for value, that is one thing. If we mean a science in which the accumulation of atomistic facts that, when put together, will ultimately provide a strong empirical warrant for all we do in classrooms, that is another. Just as teaching itself is a complex assemblage of "thats," "hows," and "tos," so too is the study of pedagogy and curriculum. "Positive" science may provide a certain, actually rather limited, amount of insight into the process. Ultimately, however, decisions in and about education are not technical, but ethical and political.[11] Whatever its glory, the history of the search for a science of education has also been the history of the transformation of educational discourse from a concern with *why* X should be taught to *how* to do it. The difficult and intensely valuative questions of content (of what knowledge is of most worth) and of teaching (of how to teach fairly and in an ethically responsive, not only efficient, manner) have been pushed to the background in our attempts to determine a set of technical procedures that will "solve " all of the problems we face.

Clearly, the report *does* recognize some of this dynamic, and in the struggle for respect and necessary resources, the notion of a science of education may be important rhetorically. After all, educators deserve respect and cannot fully succeed with the all too limited human and material resources now made available to them. However, we should not confuse the use of science as what might be called a rhetoric of justification with the much more complicated process of deliberation, conflict, and compromise that constitutes the real world of educational work.

Do not misinterpret me. There *is* a need for research. Much that goes on in classrooms *can* benefit from a closer "empirical" (interpreted as broadly as possible)[12] look and the quantitative and qualitative methods developed by social and educational researchers are essential, though not totally sufficient, tools in illuminating what is actually happening in schooling. Yet, so much of the weakest kind of educational theory and practice—overly competency based instruction, systems management, reductive accountability schemes, the construction of management systems that deskill teachers, and so on— has been justified by the claim to scientificity that I think we should be very careful of the latent effects of the current resurgence of "scientific approaches" to curriculum and teaching even when it is supported in such an articulate fashion as in *Tomorrow's Teachers*. Not only must we insist on the best of science—a commodity in rarer supply in education than we would like to admit given our propensity to borrow the reconstructed logic of science, not its logic in use[13]—but we need to avoid patterning all of education on science itself. Education is simply too ethically and politically complicated, too valuative, to be totally capturable by such a language system.

Let me repeat that even with all this said, I do have sympathy with many of the positions taken in the report. However, because of the social context in which it appears and because it has chosen to highlight certain elements in its arguments over others, its reception may signal something less than

LIBRARY
OF
MOUNT ST. MARY'S
COLLEGE
EMMITSBURG. MARYLAND

what its proponents hoped for. On a national level, the report may be used to largely justify mass testing of teachers of a very inflexible kind and a further move toward "scientific" curriculum making and competency-based teaching and teacher education. It can thereby actually depower, not empower, the very teachers the Holmes Group wishes to support.[14] At a state level, it may have the effect of reinforcing legislative intervention in the name of accountability and cost-cutting. On a local level, a number of its proposals may be used by financially troubled administrators and antagonists of teachers' unions to staff their schools with the cheapest teachers available.

These are all *possibilities*, not definites. Given the sensitivity and intelligence evident in so much of the report of the Holmes Group, and given the quality of the people involved in it, I trust that the next stages of their deliberations will take these issues into account. If they are not taken seriously, the Right, corporate America, and the efficiency experts who now pretend to be educators in the richest sense of that term will win. It will be the teachers and students who will suffer the loss. This will be at a cost that will be more than a little damaging not only to their futures but to all of ours as well.

Notes

1   For further discussion of the relationship between gender, class, and teaching, see Michael W. Apple, *Teachers and Texts: A Political Economy of Class and Gender Relations in Education* (New York: Routledge & Kegan Paul, 1987); and Sara Freedman, "Master Teacher/Merit Pay—Weeding Out Women from 'Women's True Profession,'" *Radical Teacher* 25 (November 1983): 24–28.

2   Apple, *Teachers and Texts*; and Alice Kessler-Harris, *Out to Work* (New York: Oxford University Press, 1982).

3   See Michael W. Apple, *Education and Power* (Boston: Routledge & Kegan Paul, 1982); and Andrew Gitlin, "School Structure and Teachers' Work," in *Ideology and Practice in Schooling*, ed. Michael W. Apple and Lois Weis (Philadelphia: Temple University Press, 1983), pp. 193–212.

4   Apple, *Education and Power*, especially ch. 4.

5   Apple, *Teachers and Texts*. See also Ira Shor, *Culture Wars* (New York: Routledge & Kegan Paul, 1986).

6   See Francis Fox Piven and Richard A. Cloward, *The New Class War* (New York: Pantheon Books, 1982).

7   See, for example, Robert L. Heilbroner, *The Nature and Logic of Capitalism* (New York: Norton, 1985); Joshua Cohen and Joel Rogers, *On Democracy* (New York: Penguin Books, 1983); and Martin Carnoy, Derek Shearer, and Russell Rumberger, *A New Social Contract* (New York: Harper & Row, 1983).

8   See Manuel Castells, *The Economic Crisis and American Society* (Princeton: Princeton University Press, 1980); James O'Conner, *The Fiscal Crisis of the State* (New York: St. Martin's Press, 1973); and Apple, *Education and Power*.

9   Among the best is the masterful analysis and set of proposals in Marcus Raskin, *The Common Good* (New York: Routledge & Kegan Paul, 1987). I do not fully agree with all of Raskin's proposals for education, however.

10   Francis Schrag, "Knowing and Doing," *American Journal of Education* 89 (May 1981): 253–82.

11   This is discussed in more detail in Michael W. Apple, *Ideology and Curriculum* (Boston: Routledge & Kegan Paul, 1979). See also Dwayne Huebner, "Curricular Language and Classroom Meanings," in *Language and Meaning*, ed. James B. Macdonald and Robert R. Leeper (Washington: Association for Supervision and Curriculum Development, 1966), pp. 8–26.

12   See Eric Bredo and Walter Feinberg, eds. *Knowledge and Values in Social and Educational Research* (Philadelphia: Temple University Press, 1982).

13   Abraham Kaplan, *The Conduct of Inquiry* (San Francisco: Chandler Publishing Co., 1964).

14   See Michael W. Apple and Kenneth Teitelbaum, "Are Teachers Losing Control of Their Skills and Curriculum?," *Journal of Curriculum Studies* 18 (April–June 1986): 177–84.

Reactions to *Tomorrow's Teachers*

MERLE BORROWMAN
University of California, Berkeley

Borrowman sees paradoxical tensions between the liberal and specialist parts of a teacher's education and the difficulty in nurturing a sense of creative inquiry in an educational world that is dominated by standardization of tests, curricula, and texts.

Obviously, in the Holmes Group report a distinguished set of deans, professors, and other leaders in education have given serious thought to the future of teaching in America. I have no strong disagreements with their conclusions. They make several precise recommendations, and I am particularly impressed with their sense that problems remain with respect to teacher education and teacher employment in America.

I am not surprised that my own current dean, Bernard Gifford, has been active in the Holmes Group because, in addition to his education as a scientist, he has spent much time as a political economist in such places of education as the New York City school system, the University of Rochester, and the University of California. Several members of the Holmes Group share his sense of the kinds of political and economic struggles that must be confronted. Clearly new legislation is needed, the administrative structures of school districts must be greatly modified, and the climates of opinion among teachers, students, and patrons must be changed. Moreover, the recommendations will be costly in time and money.

There are, however, some paradoxes involved in the proposals of *Tomorrow's Teachers*. For example, the Holmes Group wants the colleges in which teachers are prepared to sharply revise their general education curricula, to help potential teachers become generalists and also to insist that they carefully study the disciplines in which they will become specialists.

Jerome Bruner's recent book, *In Search of Mind: Essays in Autobiography*,[1] nicely illustrates the tensions between these two educations. As a student Bruner first experienced a liberal education, and then became a specialist as a psychologist. In much of his research he carefully followed the criteria of the discipline of psychology. However, he characterized himself as essentially a curious person who persistently "followed his nose" in the pursuit of answers to whatever general questions seemed significant to him. Most of these questions, he found, were best approached by interaction with other specialists such as anthropologists, sociologists, geologists, biologists, physicists, and philosophers. While he and his colleagues could best find answers to sharply defined small problems by diligently following their special disciplines, their major social and intellectual questions turned out to be interdisciplinary and general in nature. The pursuit of answers to these questions required dialogue.

There is a second, related problem. Bruner, and millions of other Americans, found most of his formal education boring. Students who are bright and attentive memorize the important factual data needed for short-answer class exams. Such people achieve high grade-point averages (GPAs). Since there is a vast realm of factual data, concepts, and prudential skills that every student should acquire, it is important that some accomplish this. It is hard for me to understand, however, why many people perceive this as the primary objective of formal schooling. It seems to me that the essential objective of formal schooling is to learn the arts of inquiry; hence every class should be research-oriented so far as teachers and students are concerned. I gather that Bruner would agree with me.

Indeed, I suppose that most people who produce textbooks, workbooks, curricular guides, and standardized tests would agree that inquiry is the essence of their field of study. However, if they wish to create widely used textbooks and examinations they have to "standardize" the questions raised and the answers required. Presumably, the teacher examinations that the Holmes Group believes all certified teachers must pass would be standardized. Paradoxically, having faced such standardization in their own education and professional life, teachers may well simply ask their students to memorize the expected factual responses to workbook exams and curricular guides, thereby discouraging them from personally defining the questions and finding answers to questions of greatest interest to them.

A final paradox relates to the importance of dialogue with respect to teachers. It is true, as the Holmes Group argues, that teachers are isolated, even from other teachers, and are overly controlled by pressures from community agencies, school administrators, textbook publishers, and teacher organizations. The Holmes Group hopes to minimize this problem through their system of giving three types of teacher certificates. I hope their plan works. Nevertheless, the many pressures of standardization make me pessimistic. There are of course many talented teachers who both meet the standardized expectations and are imaginative and creative with respect to how and what they teach. I gather that many of them do, openly and honestly, converse about these matters with their colleagues. But, for good reasons, most teachers do not.

Note

1 Jerome S. Bruner, *In Search of Mind: Essays in Autobiography* (New York: Harper & Row, 1984).

The Holmes Group Report:
Standards, Hierarchies, and Management

SHARON C. CONLEY
University of Arizona

SAMUEL B. BACHARACH
Cornell University

Concerned with problems of implementing the Holmes Group proposals, Conley and Bacharach explore from an organizational theory point of view issues relating to standards for entry into teaching, differential staffing models, and school management. They focus on the central issue of control vs. autonomy in the organizational structure of our schools.

The Holmes Group report, *Tomorrow's Teachers*, and the Carnegie report, *A Nation Prepared: Teachers for the 21st Century*, represent the two most serious reform documents to have appeared on the scene since the current wave of reform began four years ago. The Holmes report brings to the attention of the education community a number of critical problems and creative solutions to which other reports have given only passing attention. It has caught the imagination of both scholars and practitioners.

If the Holmes report is significant for no other reason, it is a watershed document with regard to the role of higher education in the preparation of teachers. More than any other reform report, it places much of the responsibility for improving public education on institutions of higher education and, as such, has probably kept many a department chairman and dean of education awake late into the night. The report has signaled the beginning of a new and important agenda in education reform.

This report is not, and does not pretend to be, the final word on education reform. It leaves many old agenda items unexplored and fails to deal with others. Most importantly, it has the common flaw of all such reports. While the Holmes report concentrates heavily on goals, not enough is said about strategic means for achieving these goals. Like other reports, it considers important changes in our education system, while giving little practical guidance as to the steps that must be followed to achieve the stated goals. All too often, reports such as these tend to dismiss the multiple "technical" problems that have to be considered if their goals are to be achieved. In the worthy attempt to get the message across, they often bypass the subtleties of the problems of implementation. However, if education reform is to seriously advance, we need to give these technical details careful attention within the context of possible tradeoffs.

In this article, we have chosen to deal with three issues to which we think the Holmes Group should give more elaborate consideration. It should be noted that while the Holmes report has received its greatest visibility for its emphasis on teacher preparation, in this critique we will concentrate on the report's implied structure for the teaching profession within the immediate reality of the local school district and the school.

THE NEED TO SPECIFY AN AGENDA FOR STANDARDS

Reform initiatives of the past several years have one element in common: All are concerned with "raising standards" in one way or another. Typically, they attempt to raise standards by providing incentives for practicing teachers to improve and by generating competition for scarce merit awards or promotion opportunities.[1] The "issue of standards" is directly addressed in the Holmes report's discussion concerning entry into the profession. One of the stated goals of the report is "to create standards of entry to the profession — examinations and educational requirements — that are professionally relevant and intellectually defensible" (p. 4).

Such entry standards require a set of *minimum* requirements that are designed to keep persons who fail to meet them from entering or remaining in the profession. Clearly, any profession or occupation must have a set of such standards for entry, if only because someone, somehow must make decisions about who will receive employment. But there are weaknesses inherent in any reform strategy that relies primarily or exclusively on minimum standards.

One of the problems with minimum standards is that they are readily sidestepped or lowered, whenever there are problems finding persons to bring into the profession. For instance, school districts made heavy use of emergency certificates and out-of-field assignments in the years immediately following World War II, when the nation's school districts were faced with serious staff shortages, and there is no reason to believe they will not do so again, now that another shortage is in the offing.[2] Indeed, they have already begun to make heavy use of such "exceptional" procedures to fill vacancies in mathematics and science positions. There is no reason to believe that the Holmes report recommendations, or any recommendations to date, will be able to deal with the dual goals of bringing more people into the profession and raising standards of teachers at all levels. It is critical that these dual issues be addressed.

The Holmes report appears to recognize the limited impact of minimum standards when it shifts its emphasis from standards of entry to raising standards for practicing teachers. According to the report, one of the means for assuring higher standards is a differentiated staffing system. Unfortunately, the implied system has technical difficulties of its own, which to date the Holmes Group has not addressed.

THE NEED TO SPECIFY AN AGENDA FOR DIFFERENTIATING THE PROFESSION

According to organizational theory, the purpose of differentiating staff in schools has traditionally been twofold: to give school districts special incentives to strengthen their evaluation and training procedures, and to give teachers special incentives to pay attention to evaluative feedback and to seek help in improving their performance.

The Holmes plan would create three tiers of teachers: Instructors, Professional Teachers, and Career Professionals. It appears that there would be some reduction in the amount of classroom teaching a person performs as he or she advances in the system. Teachers at the highest level would assume responsibility for new functions, such as "teacher education. . . . , curriculum improvement, testing and measurement, strengthening home-school relationships, preparing instructional materials, and conducting action research" (p. 40).

Teachers often find the concept of hierarchies initially attractive. The "flat" job structures of most school districts provide few opportunities for teachers to have a sense of career advancement or professional growth, and what opportunities they do provide involve leaving the classroom and entering administration. Ostensibly, differentiated staffing plans allow teachers to assume more responsibility for schoolwide programs, without having to leave teaching altogether.

However, the problem with specifying different levels of teachers is that there is often a tendency to immediately link levels with specific sets of responsibilities. When such a linkage is made, teachers at the lower levels of the hierarchy are inevitably assigned duties that are considered less professional or less important than those at the higher levels of the hierarchy. While the Holmes report does not explicitly suffer from the narrowness of many career ladders in this sense, it is still vulnerable to some of the same criticisms.

For example, one of the criticisms of bureaucratic career ladders is that they inevitably generate a quota system. The quota system, in turn, engenders competition for scarce rewards and disrupts the cooperation of teachers, which is so critical to education. The Holmes report does not tackle the dysfunction of an explicit or an implicit quota system. Furthermore, in leaving unclear the purpose of the hierarchy, the report leaves open two interpretations of the structure of the teaching profession: a control model and an internship model.

In the control model, each level of the hierarchy is controlled and managed by the level above it. Specifically, work is controlled by the specification of particular duties. In education, teachers would be expected to do no more and no less than the duties specified at their particular level. One of the problems with this system is that specifying that a teacher must advance to the next level before he or she is eligible to perform new and different kinds of responsibilities merely limits the number of teachers who can perform them, creating a *structural* obstacle in the system. Furthermore, specifying that particular duties "belong" to teachers at particular levels of the system virtually guarantees that advancement will be limited by quotas on the number of positions at each level, by turnover among people already in those positions, and by competition with others seeking such positions.[3]

Although intended to raise the status of teaching, a control system merely reinforces the conviction that classroom teaching itself is a less than "fully professional" activity. That is, it implies that teachers constantly need direction from those at the next higher level. An internship model, on the other hand, assumes that the purpose of hierarchies in an organization is to assure the continued development of professionals by providing them with a sense of growth, progression, and opportunity.

For example, take the case of the beginning teacher. To prepare teachers for the next level, an internship system might assign beginning teachers to work with an experienced, well-respected teacher and not immediately assign full classroom responsibilities, much in the spirit of the Holmes report. One can imagine teams of experienced teachers serving as mentors for interns and special seminars being instituted to allow interns to share their experiences, discuss common and special problems, and learn how more experienced teachers have dealt with such problems. The purpose, however, would not be to create lower-skilled jobs (so that more people in the general population would be qualified to perform them) but to assure continuous development of professional teachers at all levels.[4]

While a control model views those at the top of the hierarchy performing the function of controlling and managing the work of those below them, an internship model casts those at the top much more in a mentoring, or developmental, role. Thus, in an internship model, there is a constant emphasis on preparing teachers for the next step.

The internship model, as opposed to the control model, shows promise in addressing the dual goals of encouraging teachers to assume greater responsibility for instructional leadership and raising standards for the profession. Only the internship model is concerned with continued growth and improvement through collegiality and feedback. Finally, the internship model places a high emphasis on a critical element of any profession: the norm of self-governance.

One of the problems with the Holmes report is that it is an unclear hybrid of both models. On the one hand, one can detect uneasiness about hierarchies in the report, but on the other hand, rational, defensible reasons for having hierarchies are clearly called for. This has led to some ambiguity; for instance, it is not clear whether the primary role of the Career Professionals (third-tier teachers) is to control and manage the work of those below them, as in a control model, or to perform a development role in relation to others, as in an internship model.[5]

This is more than a theoretical debate, for in the context of a labor-management relationship and union apprehension about hierarchies, it is important that the Holmes perspective be explicitly cast within the internship framework. In future endeavors, the Holmes Group should concern itself not simply with elaborating the responsibilities of those at each career level, but also with expanding their discussion of the relationships among teachers at different levels. To date, the technical aspects of these relationships are unspecified in the Holmes report. To ignore this point is to miss one of the critical reasons that teachers have been apprehensive about hierarchies that are constructed with an unclear purpose.

Moreover, the Holmes report misses a critical point: It is not necessary to change the job structure in teaching to promote a model of internship and development. That is, there is nothing inherent in the existing job structure of public education that prevents districts from involving teachers in decision making, providing them with more developmental support, or creating internships for teachers. One does not have to create three levels in order to provide an internship for beginning teachers or to give teachers more of a leadership role and greater involvement in policy. In fact, virtually every school system in the United States already has a two-step system: the distinction between tenured and untenured teachers. Too often, however, tenure decisions are pro forma and are fraught with vague criteria. In their future efforts, the Holmes Group might give more attention to the creative use of the tenure step.[6]

THE NEED TO SPECIFY AN AGENDA
FOR SCHOOL MANAGEMENT

The Holmes report, in its emphasis on teachers, does not give enough recognition to the importance of school management as a critical component in educational productivity. In the final analysis, unless we address this issue, it will not matter how well qualified our teachers are. Placing the most highly trained teachers in poorly managed schools will get us nowhere.[7] While, implicitly, many of the suggestions made in the Holmes report are consistent with good managerial practice, the Holmes Group should be more explicit about the parameters of school management. A point that needs to be kept in mind is that colleges do not simply prepare teachers; they also prepare administrators.

Debates over the reform of school systems invariably turn on the relationship between administrators' needs for coordination and teachers' needs for discretion. All too often, administrative coordination is viewed in terms of top-down control and teacher discretion is viewed in terms of autonomy behind classroom doors. Whatever the immediate focus of attention, the implicit issue in every reform debate is always the tension between those two fundamental needs.[8]

Until recently, the issue of educational reform has rarely been stated in these terms, because those who initiate "reform" are apt to be at higher political or administrative levels, where the need for coordination is most apparent, and because they almost invariably equate coordination with limiting and controlling the discretion of those at lower levels of the system. Those at lower levels — most especially, teachers — are rarely involved in the process of formulating reform or "improvement" programs. Although sensitive to the demands of coordinating what goes on in their individual classrooms, they are most keenly aware of their own need for discretion, and frame their defense of that need in terms of autonomy from outside control.

The Holmes report begins to get us out of this dilemma by recognizing that teachers can assume many coordinative functions. However, this is only one of the horns of the dilemma. While the Holmes Group recognizes the need to give teachers more of a role in coordination, it does not give much consideration or guidance to administrators who may view the involvement of teachers in coordinative functions as a loss of administrator power.

If there are important lessons we can learn from the organizational-change literature in the private sector, it is that administrators view power as a zero sum game.[9] If we expect a high level of professionalism from our teachers, we must also expect a change in the managerial styles of those who manage teachers.

Recently, school-effectiveness research has provided some powerful clues as to what these new managerial styles might be. That research has produced evidence that schools that are demonstrably more effective than others are schools that have maximized the coordination of programs and increased the discretion of individual teachers. Although more descriptive than explanatory, the research provides general guidance as to how such schools are managed:

> Staff members have a common, coherent set of goals and objectives that they themselves have helped formulate, reflecting high expectations of themselves and their students.
>
> Principals exercise strong leadership by promoting a "norm of collegiality," minimizing status differences between themselves and their staff members, promoting informal communication, and reducing their own need to use formal controls to achieve coordination.

Principals and staff members place a high priority on staff development and continuous improvement of personal skills, promoting formal training programs, informal sharing of job knowledge, and a "norm of continuous improvement" applicable to *all* staff members.

Principals and staff members make heavy use of a variety of formal and informal processes for monitoring progress toward goals, using them to identify obstacles to such progress and ways of overcoming them, rather than using them to make summary judgments regarding the "competence" of particular staff members.

In this context, the Holmes report makes no recommendations as to how we can strengthen our programs of education administration. For too long, the discipline of education administration has been the weakest link in our schools of education. While schools of management have developed in the last ten years numerous new programs of executive training, such courses are few and far between in education. In educating administrators, schools of education should go beyond the teaching of finance and law. The time has come for us to offer first-rate programs in organizational psychology, organizational behavior, strategic management, participatory decision making, career management, and organizational culture, to name a few. If these programs of education administration are not improved, we will never be able to create the strong, cohesive organizations that can meet the challenges presented in the Holmes report.

More than any other reform report, that of the Holmes Group calls for tossing away the naive models of teaching that we have had in the past. Clearly, the Holmes Group would want teachers to develop into professional practitioners who are capable of creatively directing their students through the educational process. However, if this is to occur, we need to think about the context in which education occurs. We must begin to examine those specific changes that can be made, not simply in a profession of teaching, but in the organizational structure of our schools.

All of the reform reports have made token gestures in this direction, but we must go beyond tokenism and seriously unravel the bureaucratic complexities of our schools. These complexities include problems of evaluation, peer review, and career structures, as well as administrative and managerial processes. Our efforts must now be directed toward enhancing schools' capacities to improve, so that schools and school districts can become the primary implementors of the many recommended changes.

In the final analysis, we will be able to strengthen the abilities of school districts to deal with these complexities only by including them as partners in the reform effort. If we fail to do this, it will not matter what academic deans think, nor will it matter what research professors write. It certainly will not matter what departments of education attempt to dictate. Without bringing school districts into the reform effort, many of the recommendations made by reform groups will come to naught.

Notes

1 Samuel B. Bacharach, D. Lipsky, and Joseph Shedd, *Paying for Better Teaching: Merit Pay and Its Alternatives* (Ithaca, N.Y.: Organizational Analysis & Practice, Inc., 1984).

2 Joseph Shedd and T. Schmidle, *Teacher Shortages, Professional Standards and "Hen House" Logic* (Ithaca, N.Y.: Organizational Analysis & Practice, Inc., 1985).

3 Samuel B. Bacharach, Sharon C. Conley, and Joseph Shedd, "Beyond Career Ladders: Structuring Teachers Career Development Systems," *Teachers College Record* 87, no. 4 (Summer 1986): 563-74.

4 An analogy to this in the legal profession would be a paralegal versus a first-year lawyer.

5 Furthermore, some might claim that there is a tinge of academic elitism in the report. Indeed, if a doctoral degree becomes a requirement to establish a teacher as a Career Professional, what becomes of the role of our many non-doctoral conferring colleges?

6 Sharon C. Conley, "Performance Appraisal and Career Development Systems" (paper presented at the annual meeting of the American Educational Research Association, April 1986).

7 See Samuel B. Bacharach, Scott Bauer, and Joseph Shedd, "Education Reform and the Working Environment," *Teachers College Record* 88, no. 2 (Winter 1986): 241-56; and Samuel B. Bacharach, Scott Bauer, and Sharon C. Conley, "Organizational Analysis of Stress: The Case of Elementary and Secondary Schools," *Journal of Work and Occupations*, February 1986, pp. 7-32.

8 Samuel B. Bacharach and Sharon C. Conley, "Education Reform: A Managerial Agenda," *Phi Delta Kappan*, May 1986, pp. 641-45.

9 Samuel B. Bacharach and E. J. Lawler, *Power and Politics in Organizations* (San Francisco: Jossey-Bass, 1980).

The Holmes Group Report:
Why Reach Exceeds Grasp

LARRY CUBAN
Stanford University

Accusing the Holmes Group of selective amnesia regarding lessons learned in the earlier National Teacher Corps and Master of Arts in Teaching efforts to reform teacher education, Cuban sees their plan for action as a historically uninformed Sermon on the Mount. He also finds naive the analogy of professional development schools to teaching hospital faculty and the lack of attention paid to the politics of change in school administration.

The reach of the Holmes Group report exceeds its grasp. When it is read as a passionate call for action, I applaud. What the academics say needs saying. When it is read as an analysis of the stubborn obstacles facing professional-ization of teaching, I concur. The diagnosis of the problems is largely on target. When it is read as a reform agenda complete with strategies aimed at fundamentally changing the working conditions teachers face while improv-ing the power of students to learn, however, I get sad and annoyed.

What prompts my sadness is my heartfelt support for the Holmes Group's aims mixed with disbelief over their selective amnesia about similar efforts in previous decades. My annoyance stems from the grave flaws in their rea-soning about institutional change: They should know better.

Over two decades ago, I was a master teacher of history in a high school-based teacher education program for twenty returned Peace Corps volun-teers. Based in Washington, D.C., it was a program (in partnership with a nearby university) aimed at getting those Bachelor of Arts in Teaching grad-uate with overseas experience a Master of Arts in Teaching degree within twelve months while equipping them to survive in tough schools. I taught two classes a day, and observed and critiqued four interns (who also taught two classes). University faculty taught afternoon seminars at the high school. All of us, including the other master teachers in English and Math and their interns, performed a tripartite role: teach students, develop curriculum materials, and work after school with students and their families or in the community.

The Cardozo Project in Urban Teaching, named after the high school in which it was initially located, became the working model for the National Teacher Corps in 1966. For the next fifteen years, there was a federally funded effort to revitalize teacher education, invigorate urban teaching through conceptualizing a different role for teachers, and alter schooling for poor children and those of color. Tens of thousands of teachers were trained in schools across the country. Thousands of university faculty enlisted. Scores of research reports and studies were written. No reference to these experiences (or, for that matter, the Ford Foundation's millions that were spent on fifth-year programs in the 1950s and 1960s) appear in any of the report's discussions on teacher education, professional development schools, or staff differentiation.

Hard lessons learned from these earlier efforts in university-school collaboration and repeated forays into organizational change would have been instructive for subsequent calls for reform. The absence of references to previous relevant, large-scale programs to point out earlier flaws in conception, execution, or institutional barriers suggests a long-term memory loss.

What further annoyed me was the unblushing innocence of the proposed strategies and solutions offered in the face of so many previous efforts to alter teacher education programs, schools, and classrooms. Space limits prevent more than a brief discussion of three features of this innocence:

> Changing three basic elements in mature, interlocking educational institutions (state certification, university practices and attitudes toward teaching, and working conditions within school systems) from the insecure perch of schools of education within research universities
>
> The serious flaws in comparing medical practice to teaching
>
> An absence of understanding that fundamental alterations in schools are linked to what administrators believe and do

CHANGING FEATURES IN THREE INSTITUTIONS

Trying to alter certification policies and working conditions in schools requires, at the very least, mobilizing large bipartisan coalitions that include both lay and professional groups aimed at state legislatures, governors, and state superintendents. No easy task, such political efforts require the right circumstances, much money, and staying power. While it would be beyond the scope of the report to lay out a specific strategy, recognition of the political dimensions of the task ahead would have satisfied at least one reader that the authors were aware of the awesome magnitude of their mission. I found little such awareness in the report other than the ringing statement that the group "is committed to carrying the reform of teacher education into the classroom by establishing strong linkages with schools; into the central office and boardroom by working with local school systems; and into the state legislative chamber by working for changes in the policies that shape the teaching profession" (p. 62). In stating their intent, what the authors call a "program of action" is simply a plea (p. 19).

The rhetoric of pleading becomes far more evident when the report sticks to what they know best: the research university. Here the authors want the undergraduate curriculum to be transformed "so that future teachers can study the subjects they will teach with instructors who model fine teaching and who understand the pedagogy of their material" (p. 16). Moreover, academic requirements need to be overhauled so that "undergraduate students can gain a sense of the intellectual structure and boundaries of their disciplines" (p. 16). Such changes would require top university officials to champion the reforms and "unprecedented cooperation" (p. 18) among faculty. Both would somehow appear in the face of research universities' explicit reward systems that oppose such directions. That is, teaching is secondary at most of these places; research productivity is primary. Furthermore, the study and practice of education is often seen as low status and intellectually questionable. Their first move to invite chief academic officers is sensible, of course, but far more will need to be done. Perhaps, those details and steps to alter university reward systems and the academic pecking order are yet to come. I hope so.

I endorse the authors' goals. I yearn for these outcomes. But the part of me that has spent a quarter century in public schools and five years at one such research institution asks: how? I no longer want a Sermon on the Mount.

COMPARING MEDICAL EDUCATION TO TEACHER EDUCATION

This popular analogy again has surfaced in the drive to boost public respect for teaching through raising entrance and recertification standards for both newcomers and veterans.

I believe that such a direction in certifying experienced teachers through a series of practical and written examinations that link results to differentiated staffing is both sensible and worth pursuing. Such certification procedures exist in a number of professions.

But when the authors speak of professional development schools and openly compare such settings with teaching hospitals, I argue, on the basis of my experience in such settings two decades ago, for closer examination of the analogy. A professional development school would bring teachers and administrators "together with university faculty in partnerships that improve teaching and learning on the part of their respective students" (p. 56). Unlike university laboratory schools, "these are 'real world' schools and as often as possible include pupils from disadvantaged homes" (p. 88). Such sites have two immediate purposes: training prospective professionals and generating new knowledge and better practice. The latter purpose implies experimentation. Overall, these professional development schools would be the primary tool employed in changing the structure and working conditions in schools.

I endorse the first purpose but question the second because of the unique obligation that schools have and teaching hospitals lack: Students are compelled to go to school; you choose to enter a teaching hospital.

In a teaching hospital, the emphasis is as much on doctors' learning as it is on providing services to patients. Sick people with exotic illnesses and terminal diseases encourage use of experimental treatments. Resident and intern doctors, under the supervision of both clinical and research faculty, run the basic services, learning from their errors in treatment and incomplete knowledge. In all cases, however, patients who voluntarily enter must give permission for nonstandard treatments.

Public schools differ. Compulsory attendance produces a unique set of expectations and obligations encased in judicial decisions about what teachers and principals can and cannot do. Awareness of this seems to be missing from the report. These professional development schools are responsible to a school board, which is responsible to the community. Introducing new curricula, pedagogy, classroom arrangements, and the like (especially in low-income areas where historically experiments have occurred without much disclosure) would, at some level, need informed consent of the parents of students and the school board. Of course, these proposed centers could be made into alternative schools where parents choose to send their children but then those unseemly echoes of laboratory schools and atypical students would probably arise from critics.

The point is that the Holmes Group is either unwilling or unaware of the need to subject the medical metaphor to closer scrutiny. For wrapped within the analogy is a strategy of planned change: the lighthouse school. The notion of an exemplary school governed by a district and a university that produces new working arrangements and professional practices is a familiar tactic undertaken numerous times in earlier reform efforts. It has obvious strengths but contains serious limitations in design that have surfaced in earlier decades. As a strategy to alter working conditions for teachers in all of a district's schools, it would take at least a decade-long commitment from a university. Such unawareness or unwillingness to examine more carefully the medical analogy and the strategy for change embedded within it weakens in my mind the obvious strengths of the report.

ADMINISTRATORS AND CHANGE IN SCHOOLS

The report evidences a lack of understanding that fundamental alterations in schools are linked to political changes outside schools and must, in basic ways, take into account what administrators believe and do. An explicit goal of the Holmes Group is to make schools better places for teachers to work and learn. The authors state that such an aim requires "less bureaucracy, more professional autonomy, and more leadership for teachers" (p. 4). If research into the results of planned changes in schools over the last half-century has shown anything it is that basic changes in the organizational structures are necessary prior steps in any sustained effort to touch what teachers do daily in classrooms. The common school movement in the mid-nineteenth century, the progressives at the turn of the century, the 1960s, and the current moment of reform all began outside of the schools and were profoundly political, that is, aimed toward particular larger social goals. In all cases, they had limited impact on classroom instruction and administrative behavior when the structural arrangements within which both teachers and administrators worked were not altered.

Initiating professional development schools, regardless of their efficacy, is a long-term strategy committed to demonstrating to others that research will produce knowledge that will convince others to alter their unenlightened ways. Unless the presidents and deans of major private and public universities will enlist in a major national campaign aimed at enlisting corporate sponsors, legislators at the state and national levels, and similar groups, such a strategy of introducing occasional schools around the country strikes me as embarrassingly naive. Unsurprisingly, such a rational view of organizational change emanates from the academy.

Moreover, if expanding the leadership of teachers is desired, what are the implications for principals and superintendents? To expand the zone of discretion for one has ripple effects on the others because the organizational positions are wired together (albeit to different degrees of tautness in organizations). No such awareness of how principals and superintendents (forgetting school boards, for the moment—if one can) are deeply immersed in any intentional effort to alter what teachers do intrudes into the discussion. The research literature on the importance of administrators is unambiguous on their centrality to planned change. The legal delegation of authority from the state to a local school district to run schools goes in a clear line from the school board and superintendent to principals. Clearly, there are many ways that administrators and teachers can work together within districts and schools, but inattention to their pivotal role leaves me wondering if I am dealing in slogans or Alice-in-Wonderland reverie rather than thoughtful analysis.

The major points that I make in these comments deal with excess. The goals of the Holmes Group are noble. Schools of education at research universities can, indeed, have an impact on schooling in the nation through the training they do of most teacher educators. If they were to concentrate on altering the university curriculum and lessening academic inattentiveness to teaching and succeed, that in itself would constitute a major victory. I, for one, would enlist in that campaign. To promise major changes in school structures and teaching practices through those university reforms, state recertification policies, and professional development schools, however, exceeds the grasp of how organizational arrangements within schools have persisted over time.

The Holmes Group report is part of another search for ways of improving what happens within schools. As with other reports promising a heaven on earth, expectations may soar. Inflated claims, like snippets of film reviews that hype a motion picture, block serious analysis of persistent issues in public schooling. What the Holmes Group proposes for revisions in the university and for differentiated careers is a worthwhile agenda that would take at least a decade, at the minimum, to achieve.

Why present teacher education reforms that must be achieved initially within the university as a central thrust for a fundamental reform in public schooling? One possible answer is that the rhetoric of reform in this culture forces a style on national reports: We have a crisis; here is the problem; here is what needs to be done; go do it. All of this to be done in spare, clear prose. Why?

I have a hunch. My guess is that the people who write such reports (and I have done my share) often believe that excess is what gains public notice; moderation in tone and word glazes the eye and loses attention. Simplicity is preferred over complexity. This is a television formula for a half-hour program applied to national reports although there are undoubtedly other possible explanations for what I see in the report as a mystifying innocence about fundamental change in school processes and an exaggerated view of the role universities can play in that change.

Modesty and humility, neglected attributes in most reformers, seem appropriate even in the face of Browning's question about exceeding one's grasp: "Or, what's a heaven for?" Schooling has been afflicted with too many "heavens" over the last century. The Holmes Group report has within it proposals for important changes within the university. That is an appropriate starting point. It will take much time and sustained effort just to achieve the aims they have set for themselves. While they must stay involved in state certification policies, lobbying legislatures for changes, and while they should continue partnerships with school districts, the centerpiece of their efforts should be clearly on where they work daily. That strikes me as a tough, unrelenting set of worthwhile tasks that will take time and fortitude. If they do so, reach and grasp will come together.

Schools for Tomorrow's Teachers

LINDA DARLING-HAMMOND
The Rand Corporation, Washington, D.C.

Declaring that "the foundation of a profession is not permission to practice autonomously, it is shared responsibility for collectively shaping standards of professional practice," Linda Darling-Hammond speaks to the differential staffing and professional development school proposals of the Holmes Group. However, her central concern is with the nature of good teaching itself.

The most eloquent statements in the Holmes Group report are those that describe good teaching:

> [Competent teachers] possess broad and deep understanding of children, the subjects they teach, the nature of learning and schooling, and the world around them. They exemplify the critical thinking they strive to develop in students, combining tough-minded instruction with a penchant for inquiry. . . . Competent teachers are careful not to bore, confuse, or demean students, pushing them instead to interact with important knowledge and skill. Such teachers interpret the understandings students bring to and develop during lessons; they identify students' misconceptions, and question the surface responses that mask true learning. . . . Truly competent teachers find it as important to discover ways of helping those who find learning difficult and frustrating as they do helping those who find school learning easy and rewarding. . . . For competent professionals, students' learning is the *sine qua non* of teaching and schooling. (pp. 28–29)

In statements such as this one, the group offers its most cogent rationale for its proposals to strengthen teacher education: that good teaching requires far more than the ability to deliver lectures to faceless listeners. It requires knowledge of and insight into the minds of students, and relentless imagination in forging connections that will make understanding the possession of the learner, not just the teacher. Such knowledge, insight, and imagination do not spring full-blown from the minds of liberally educated college students like Athena from the forehead of Zeus. They must be developed and nurtured through careful and disciplined inquiry, practice, and reflection.

It is hoped that later reports of the Holmes Group will offer more discussion of the attributes of good teaching and the means by which it can be encouraged and supported. At the moment, the group's published statements are tantalizing but still vague on this score, and perhaps too specific in some other respects.

A great deal of attention is paid to defining differentiated titles and roles for teachers and to describing the education and testing requirements for these positions. Instructors would have to pass tests of reading, writing, subject matter, general knowledge, and the "rudiments of pedagogy" after graduating from college. They would have little or no autonomy in the classroom, being supervised by Career Professionals. Professional Teachers would complete a master's degree in teaching; after passing all of the aforementioned tests, plus examinations in pedagogy and learning, they would be allowed to plan their own lessons and teach without supervision. Career Professionals — expected to comprise about 20 percent of the teaching force — would be allowed to participate in school-level decision making and supervision after completing the equivalent of a doctoral degree and passing "professional practice examinations" in their areas of specialization.

All of this hierarchy is intended to ensure that those licensed to make decisions about their own and others' teaching are sufficiently prepared to do so. This is an important aim deserving special emphasis at a time when teacher shortages and disaffection with teacher education are persuading some policymakers to allow certification and hiring of individuals not trained to teach. But the imposition of multiple testing requirements and the creation of new slots in school bureaucracies are formalistic responses to a far more profound problem. How can we create schools in which teaching will be given first priority and the expertise of teachers will be honored?

I am not convinced that creating an inflexible hierarchy of teachers, in which roles are determined exclusively by credentials, will solve the larger problem. In any occupation, credentials are at best an indication of what individuals might be expected to know. Credentials can never fully represent what people of diverse talents and temperaments are actually able and willing to do. Designations of teachers' roles and responsibilities in schools ought to be based largely on demonstrated aptitude and performance. As in other walks of life, using test scores and grade-point averages (GPAs) to decide who should do what will reinforce the Peter Principle in some cases and underemploy individual capabilities in others. Given the magnitude of the job that must be done, we do not have the luxury of squandering teaching talent by limiting its use on the basis of poor proxies for ability that can never really capture the demands of the work and the potential of diverse workers. We need to effectively use all of the teaching talents available in schools if we are to produce better schools and more able learners.

Of most concern here is the thinking that only the 20 percent of teachers who have satisfied all of the formal requirements for Career Professional status will be permitted to engage in professional activities, such as supervision, curriculum development, and school-level policymaking. If other "professional" teachers are barred from such activities, they will have been misnamed, for the foundation of a profession is not permission to practice autonomously, it is shared responsibility for collectively shaping standards of professional practice. Once certified, professionals must be expected to assume this responsibility. The avenues for contributing to improvement of practice are many and varied; they need not be bureaucratized and credential-bound. Rather than professionalizing teaching, this vision of a titled and privileged elite reinforces the status quo of top-down management in schools and undermines a truly professional conception of most teachers' work.

Until well-educated teachers are permitted and expected to jointly define and structure their collective work, schools will remain knowledge factories, with teachers expected to "process" students in egg-crate classrooms where apparent autonomy is constrained by predetermined technical controls. Responsibility for shaping schooling must permeate the teaching force, or schools will not change in substantial ways.

The easiest thing we can ask school systems to do is to add another specialized slot to their existing bureaucracies. The hardest thing to accomplish is the transformation of teaching and learning from a rule-following exercise to a real engagement of creative minds bent on understanding rather than on acquisition of testable facts.

Accomplishing the latter probably does require one of the distinctions made by the Holmes Group. By distinguishing Instructors from Professional Teachers, the deans make an important inroad into the problem of how to deregulate teaching. Teaching can ultimately become responsive to students' needs and to the demands of intellectually honest learning if the public can be convinced that teachers are sufficiently expert to be released from rules prescribing what will be taught when and how. So long as people who know little about teaching are accorded full status as teachers, politicians will feel compelled to tell teachers what to do. It is only by regulating *teachers* that we will be able to deregulate *teaching*.

The report does a fine job of debunking the "bright-person" myth of teaching, which rests on the assumption that anyone who knows a subject is automatically able to teach that subject to all sorts of students in all sorts of settings. The real job of teaching is not fashioning accurate lectures that will be understood by some students under ideal conditions. It is figuring out what lots of different students know, how they have come to understand the world, how they learn, and how they might be motivated and engaged to develop richer understandings and keener perceptions of the areas under study. This is not easy work. It is not made easier by standardized curricular guidelines and packaged lessons; it is simply ignored.

Given that individuals who are not fully prepared to undertake the whole job of teaching may still want to teach, and in any event, will continue to be hired by schools, the Holmes Group proposes that they be hired as Instructors and supervised by Professional Teachers. Some will, as is traditionally the case, teach for only a few years and go on to other pursuits. Others may choose to acquire the preparation necessary for full status as a Professional Teacher. The important thing is that they will not be left unaided in the development of teaching skill, and their students will not be left unprotected during the necessary learning period.

This is an important idea, one that will strengthen the teaching profession and provide the basis for increasing Professional Teachers' control over the structure and substance of their work. There are, of course, expenses implicit in this supervisory model, but these are paltry in comparison with the continued costs — both financial and educational — of encouraging learned incompetence through unsupervised sink-or-swim induction, thus reinforcing a teacher-proof approach to school management. The expenses of supervising untrained novices would also provide an incentive for school systems to hire more professionally trained teachers. The benefits would be the presumption of teacher competence needed to legitimize professional control over technical decisions regarding teaching.

There is a real-world hitch in this vision of a differentiated teaching force in which experts transmit their knowledge to novices. Whether one envisions three tiers of teachers or two, the most expert of teachers — and the least well-prepared — are not equally distributed across schools and districts of different types. The most highly trained teachers are found disproportionately in schools that offer attractive working conditions and salaries and that provide the most capable school leadership.

Due to a combination of predictable labor-market forces, seniority rules for teacher transfers, and high rates of attrition in difficult schools, those schools with the largest numbers of new and untrained teachers typically have the fewest well-trained teachers. These also tend to be schools serving less-advantaged students, who pose greater challenges to school staff. The result is that the fewest resources for supervision and school improvement exist in those schools that need them most.

There is a potential answer to this widespread problem in the Holmes Group's proposal for professional development schools, intended to link universities and school systems in the common cause of improving knowledge about teaching, training new entrants, and developing more effective approaches to teaching and schooling. Creating such schools in the places where most new teachers are employed and where such resources are most needed would be a giant step toward the professionalization of teaching and the improvement of education.

Incentives to attract highly expert teachers to these schools would be inherent in the opportunities for experimentation and collective problem solving offered by "providing teachers with opportunities to contribute to the development of knowledge in their profession, to form collegial relationships beyond their immediate working environment, and to grow intellectually as they mature professionally" (p. 56).

If we can create professional development schools that are indeed professionally designed and operated, that push the edges of teaching knowledge forward, and that support both good teaching and good teacher education on behalf of students most in need of inspired and capable instruction, we will have made a profound contribution to real and lasting educational reform. We do not need highly elaborated credentialing procedures to make a start in this direction. We need enlightened leadership on the part of teachers, school administrators, and teacher educators, and support from legislators and school boards. The Holmes Group can lead the way as they continue their search for wedges to open the door to a more professional structure for teaching. Of the many paths they could next pursue, I hope they choose this one.

Comments on *Tomorrow's Teachers*

ROBERT DREEBEN
University of Chicago

Can education be improved by improving teacher education without taking into account the many other forces that impinge on the quality of education? Probably not, is Dreeben's conclusion. Regarding the Holmes Group report, he concludes that the proposed differential staffing is merely a new set of names for the kind of staffing we already have: substitute and nontenured teachers, tenured teachers, and administrators — and that what we are really witnessing in this and other reform proposals is an underlying political debate of major proportions regarding the educational role of the state and our conceptions of the public and the private.

The Holmes Group report aims to improve the quality of education by improving the quality of teachers (p. 23). To justify this remedy (making teachers better) it argues that (presumably good) "curriculum plans, instructional materials, elegant classrooms, and even sensitive and intelligent administrators cannot overcome the negative effects of weak teaching" (p. 23). But what of the converse? Can good teachers overcome the negative effects of poor plans, instruction, and administration? Does the argument run both ways? The second question is not so congruent with the commitments of deans of schools of education to "reform . . . teacher education" (p. 3), and "to change the teaching profession" (p. 5) as is the first. It opens the door to remedies that originate outside the jurisdiction of schools of education.

If the main goal of the report is to improve education, then its remedy, in addition to being slightly parochial, begs the question. It takes on faith the primacy of teacher quality and fails to pose open questions about how curricular, instructional, and administrative considerations contribute to educational outcomes. It might have asked: What cluster of conditions must be changed, including teacher quality, for education to improve? It implicitly relegates these other considerations to a residual category of working conditions (presumably those becoming to professionals) without attending to how they are entailed in teaching.

The report reifies teaching, abstracts it not only from its surroundings, particularly the local arrangements for providing education, but also from the resources that sustain it. While responding to the prevailing political climate, it proceeds from no analysis of schooling, of school system organization, or of teaching as an occupation. This observation does not deny that the quality of teaching needs improvement; rather, it raises the question of whether educational improvement can be narrowly restricted to teaching while other forces that contribute to the quality of education remain neglected.

The Holmes Group remedy aims to change the occupation so that work in it will become more intellectually challenging, better paying, less demeaning, and more careerlike. The differentiation of teaching is the key principle for accomplishing these ends. Accordingly, the report envisions a threefold division of job categories: (1) Career Professionals ("experts in a specialized area, such as curriculum development, teacher evaluation, or school management" [p. 8]), the "top practitioners" charged with "lead[ing] their field to improvement" and with supporting and supervising Instructors (novices at teaching); (2) Professional Teachers ("who have proven their competence at work, in rigorous professional qualification examinations, and in their own education" [p. 8]); and (3) Instructors ("bright college graduates with a solid academic background in one or two subjects, . . . who could pass an entrance exam" [p. 9] as well as knowledgeable adults from other walks of life qualified to provide instruction).

Is this not, however, a familiar cast of characters differing from the status quo mainly in the novelty of the titles? Specialists in curriculum, management, and supervision, holding higher degrees, already populate the middle and upper levels of school system administration and the faculty ranks of schools of education. Note that such people are not strictly speaking part of the teaching profession; they are administrators and academics. The Holmes Group, however, metamorphoses them into teachers: Career Professionals will hold "jobs in which fine teachers can use their pedagogical expertise to improve other teachers' work, as well as to help children" (p. 8). How they will continue to be teachers and at the same time specialize in curriculum, manage, supervise, and lead the profession — tasks that draw them out of the classroom and in some respects put them in conflict with the interests of teachers — is not spelled out.

What the Holmes Group leaves out of consideration, in its preoccupation with teacher quality, is that public education is organized hierarchically at the local level where communities pay taxes to have a service performed and regulated. People who currently resemble what the Holmes Group calls Career Professionals (i.e., administrators) do this regulation, and teachers who want to do this sort of work and thereby increase their challenge, responsibility, and pay as well as extend their careers in education characteristically renounce their jobs as teachers, get a higher degree, and join the ranks of administrators. Those who want to achieve these career gains on the academic side also leave teaching to join academia. Who, then, will the Career Professionals be? To whom will they owe their positions: to school systems, to universities, to an association (currently not existing) that regulates the occupation at large? And from what source will they derive power and authority to effect change in the work of teachers?

The report does not address how a presumed elite cadre can be kept within the bounds of the occupation. Some occupations have solved this problem by merging the training of new members and the generation of new knowledge and technique with the day-to-day performance of work. Teaching has not succeeded in doing this in good measure because school systems as public utilities do not regard the kind of activities that universities do in training and research as part of their mission.

The Professional Teacher bears a striking resemblance to the current teacher with tenure: the holder of an acceptable academic qualification whose competence has been judged satisfactory in an authorized fashion. Most likely the Holmes Group would object to my equating Professional Teachers with current tenured teachers: The latter it treats as part of the problem and the former as a solution to it. The difference would lie, from its perspective, in the more "serious educational requirements, and in the stiff standards for entry to and continuance in teaching" (pp. 8–9) so that only the bright and highly qualified could enter. The key issues, however, revolve around adjudicating the conflicting claims for higher entry standards with conditions in the labor market for teachers, and effecting changes in the activities of teachers to accomplish better educational outcomes. Recommending higher standards does not join those issues.

The size of the Professional Teacher contingent and the extent to which the qualifications and competence of the teaching force are actually increased will depend on how high the threshold for entry is set and how large the contingent of Instructors (the new name for untenured teachers, full-time substitutes, temporary teachers, etc.) will be. The size of both will be influenced by the fluctuating demand for teachers, that for the less qualified increasing with teacher demand. As that demand shifts, the proportion of qualified instructors will vary — as it always has — because education is a labor-intensive public utility. The "warm body" problem will exist as long as we wait for a pedagogically sound way to instruct many more students per class than we now can accommodate. And while the report states that its new arrangement would "absorb enrollment swings without the mindless" hiring and laying-off of new teachers (p. 9), no solution is actually suggested beyond asserting the anticipated competence of the novice Instructors. It is not clear why hiring Instructors, whose duration on the job is defined in the report as short-term, will be different from what happens now except, of course, in language: Instructors rather than untenured teachers will be laid off and hastily hired.

There is much less in these proposed reforms than meets the eye. In an overelaborate way, the Holmes Group asks for the raising of academic credentials for entry without indicating how this will contribute to greater competence. Mobility in education will still mean leaving the teaching ranks, and the occupation will still have to be responsive to fluctuations in the size of the school-age population from place to place. The great stress on standards, academic and work performance, however, will no doubt indicate to the public that educators take improvement seriously and want to do something about the alleged parlous state of education. That would not be a bad outcome, but it should not be confused with improving the profession or education, or at least not with improving them much.

The recommendations of the Holmes Group report are not limited to reorganizing the categories of the occupation; they extend to the preparation of teachers, a task "distinctively the province of the university" (p. 20). The core of the reform will be to replace the undergraduate major in education with majors in the subjects of instruction, even at the elementary level. Whatever the merits of this proposal, it suggests a reconstitution of elementary school organization and curriculum in a more departmentalized direction. (Secondary schools are already departmentalized.) The latter is a development that will require new thinking about methods of instruction and ability grouping in perhaps more than one subject, about the coherence of curricular sequences over successive school years, and about the nature of the supervisory apparatus in schools and school systems. Departmentalization in elementary schools might be a good or a bad idea, but the report does not address it — another example of its reluctance to open up the educational improvement question broadly and of its proclivity to settle, prematurely, in my view, on the teacher-quality remedy.

The report briefly discusses changes in universities designed to improve teachers and education. The first two changes call for improving undergraduate instruction by providing "greater coherence and dedication to the historic tenets of liberal education" so "essential to improving teacher education" (p. 47) and changing "course requirements and courses so that undergraduate students can gain a sense of the intellectual structure and boundaries of their disciplines" (p. 16). Here, man bites dog: Those who would speak for teachers complain about the universities, a turnabout from the customary and tiresome academic squawking that freshmen arrive at college unprepared. More seriously, the report advocates tackling an equally (perhaps more) grandiose and intractable problem, the reform of undergraduate education, as a means to improve primary and secondary education. The notion that teachers' skills are shaped by the allegedly inadequate performance of their own teachers earlier rests on an evidentiary base of folklore, far less than what would be required to justify the overhaul of undergraduate education in the interest of improving public school instruction. Somewhat more precise procedural reasoning might have been expected here.

The third change comes closer to the report's avowed goal: to design programs of research and training that will support the development of subject-specific pedagogy and the evaluation of instruction (p. 17). There can be no quarrel with this in general; indeed, such a research agenda is already in progress, though regrettably the weight of this work has not increased in anywhere near the same proportion as its volume. As a major recommendation of the report, however, it represents only the mildest injunction for the improvement of education—an item on the Holmes Group's forthcoming agenda.

In particular, however, some quarrel is appropriate, and it pertains to what I have already identified as the report's preoccupation with the quality of teaching. A major limitation of ongoing research on instruction and pedagogy has been its single-minded emphasis on teachers' characteristics, strategies, patterns of interaction with students, conceptions, and modes of thought. The influence on the educational process of the properties of classes, schools, and school systems as they impinge on instruction through the distribution of student characteristics, the selection and use of curricular materials, and the allocation and use of time at different layers of the school system have suffered from relative neglect. The report's research agenda, so heavily weighted toward pedagogy—a matter of importance when not treated in isolation—and teacher learning, does not hold great promise, in my estimation, for the improvement of education because of what it excludes. On the research side, the report in effect proposes doing more of what we have been doing.

Teaching entails the utilization of educational resources that both enable instruction to occur and constrain it. Otherwise excellent teaching can be hamstrung by poorly conceived textbooks fashioned by publishers, ill-advised book acquisition policies by school systems, inadequate allocations of time to curricular areas, destructive scheduling, inappropriate assignments of students to classes and tracks, and the like. The remedies for these educational inadequacies do not usually lie in the improvement of teachers but in understanding how classroom events are shaped by curricular choices made in the central offices of school systems, how district time priorities are respecified in schools and classrooms, and how both time and curricular knowledge are adapted to the capacities of different aggregates of students. No amount of renaming the categories of teachers or stiffening entrance examinations to the occupation is going to provide remedies for problems in how school systems allocate and use the resources for mounting instructional programs.

There are, of course, matters of pedagogy (instruction) that fall within the province of teachers, but they do not lie solely there because teachers are part of a larger enterprise and do not cut their work out of whole cloth. Teacher improvement is necessary, but in the context of knowing something about the nature of the larger educational setting into which the work of teachers is inextricably tied. This requires, in addition to improving the working conditions that teacher organizations identify as influencing the dignity of work, taking into account the origin and allocation of educational resources in school systems that form the components of teachers' instructional efforts.

The Holmes Group report lacks a diagnostic analysis of the schooling process. It does not lead us in the direction of understanding the nature of the educational enterprise and of the place of teachers within it, considerations that in my view should be at the heart of educational reform. It does not provide the steps in reasoning that show how redividing the occupation of teaching and revising teacher preparation will eventuate in productive changes in educational organization and in the activities of teaching.

For schooling to be improved, instruction must be improved. Part of that improvement will have to come from teachers; another part will have to come from those who staff the middle and upper reaches of school systems. Universities and schools of education will have their contributions to make, as will book publishers and teacher organizations. Little improvement will occur without identifying how the activities of these groups shape the organization and practice of instruction.

Providing those in the education business with a new set of job titles and making entry into the higher levels of the occupation and their improved salaries depend on tests and credentials might persuade taxpayers to relax their grip on the public purse to some extent. Beyond that, it is hard to see how the Holmes Group remedies will improve schooling much beyond denying entry to a small number of incompetent teachers and attracting a small number of teachers who will find teaching marginally more attractive than some prevailing alternative — both being desirable though limited ends. The report addresses itself more to modifying the image of teaching by proposing changes in publicly visible job classifications and entrance standards than to how school systems, not just teachers, provide instruction and how they can do it better.

All this having been said, discussing the report as a document on teacher and school improvement, as I have done, to some extent misses the point. It has a meaning distinct from its explicit content. This report, along with others making similar recommendations, appears at a historical moment of educational controversy over the soul of education and, perhaps more importantly, over money and government policy. The Holmes Group's position bears a strong resemblance, for example, to that argued by the Carnegie Forum Task Force on Teaching as a Profession, *A Nation Prepared*, and by the Committee for Economic Development, *Investing in Our Children*.[1]

The specific content and recommendations of these reports are less important than their underlying agenda to support public schools as publicly financed institutions under state control dedicated to the generation and transmission of secular and universalistic knowledge for secular ends. The reports are the product of a loose coalition of professionals, business leaders, and universities, the traditional repositories of these values. They stand in general opposition to those who support the infusion of religious values into the public domain, the public support of private institutions, and local definitions of what constitutes knowledge.

We are witnessing a political debate of major dimensions. The improvement of schools may get lost in the shuffle because most of the remedies speak to the political agenda. It matters greatly, however, how this debate is resolved; and the issue of school improvement may be of less importance in the broader scheme to things.

Note

1 Committee for Economic Development, *Investing in Our Children* (New York: Committee for Economic Development, 1985).

The Holmes Group Report and the Professionalization of Teaching

WALTER FEINBERG

The University of Illinois, Urbana

Critical of the economic orientation and assumptions of the Carnegie report, Feinberg finds the Holmes Group report less problematic. Nevertheless, he raises questions about liberal and professional studies, secondary and primary teachers, professional hierarchy, similarities to medical education, and the relation of schooling to social-economic problems.

It is not difficult to be excited about the Holmes Group report and to admire its bold attempt to restructure teacher education. In response to criticism from outside of the profession, the Holmes Group proposes to abolish undergraduate teacher education programs, to require that all future teachers have a liberal arts major, and to reestablish teacher education as a graduate program. In response to criticism from within the university, it points to the importance of a broad, liberal education for all teachers while expressing concern that the quality of instruction in the liberal arts needs to be improved. In its response to recent criticisms of the teaching profession, the Holmes report also attempts to provide a rationale for the different components of teacher education. For example, to counter the view that anyone who knows a subject well can teach it, the report points to the special needs of high-risk populations of students and argues that proficiency in the theory and skills of pedagogy are necessary components of teacher education. In its recommendation for the establishment of professional development schools, the analogue of medical education's teaching hospitals, the Holmes Group provides a potentially sound way to ground these different components of teacher education in a sustained and controlled teaching environment.

Perhaps even more important than its specific recommendations, the Holmes Group offers a renewed image of the teacher, an image that serves as a strong response to much of the recent criticism of teaching. Professional teachers are to be active agents in the teaching process and not simply conduits transmitting skills, behaviors, or attitudes to a group of children through the use of prescribed materials. Rather, Professional Teachers, when properly trained, will be able to evaluate and pass judgment on the transmission process. They will be able to challenge the advice of "experts" and knowledgeably advance the cause of individual students. Moreover, they will be able to do this out of the sense of confidence that comes from a clear understanding of a child's needs and of the effective ways in which to meet them.

HOLMES AND CARNEGIE

In evaluating the Holmes report, it is important to distinguish it from another proposal for reform issued at about the same time—the Carnegie Forum's Task Force on Education and the Economy, entitled *A Nation Prepared*. The two reports make a number of similar recommendations that are worth serious consideration, but there are also important differences. As its title indicates, the Carnegie report is intended as a response to the earlier report of the President's Commission on Excellence in Education, entitled *A Nation at Risk*. As such, it follows that earlier document by focusing on what it claims to be the link between education and the economy. While the report gestures to other functions of schooling, such as developing an informed citizenry and assuring equal opportunity, its primary focus is on the importance of a renewed teaching profession in helping the nation to meet the economic challenges it describes. Thus whereas the Holmes Group has provided a report about the educational needs of the teaching profession and the structural changes that must be made to meet them, the Carnegie Forum has provided a statement about the competitive position of the United States in the international market and has elaborated the educational changes that improving this position would entail.

This is an important difference and raises certain questions about the content of the Carnegie report that need not be raised about the Holmes document. For example, the basic point of the Carnegie report is that dull, routine, repetitive work is moving to other areas of the world because American workers are no longer willing to do such work for the wages that workers in other countries are willing to accept. This means that if American labor is to be competitive in the years ahead, it will have to engage in highly technical activity requiring a good deal of intellectual training. Hence schools, which once were content to teach by drill and routine and to develop habits appropriate to the assembly line, now need to be teaching more abstract skills and more flexible patterns of behavior. More than ever, the report tells us, students will be required to think rather than simply to follow the directions of others. The plausibility of the Carnegie recommendations therefore depends on the accuracy of its assessment of the future economic needs of the country. However, the fact that it fails to address research showing that a substantial number of jobs will continue to require rather routine skills significantly detracts from the case it is trying to make.[1]

An even more serious problem with the Carnegie report is the way in which it describes the movement of labor. American labor is pictured as simply unwilling to work for the low wages that foreign workers are eager to accept. The reader is told of Korean workers who produce video recorders for the American market working seven days a week, twelve hours a day, for $3,000 a year and is warned that as long as "products and services can be produced by people with low skills who are willing to work hard for relatively low wages, the technology and capital will move to their doorstep" (p. 12). What the Carnegie report does not mention is that it is very difficult to tell whether Koreans are willing to work for $.67 an hour because the organizations through which their voices could be expresesed, such as unions, are essentially illegal. It also neglects to mention that one important reason serious union activity is banned is because, should Korean workers demand too much in the way of wages, capital could flow again to other countries where wages are lower, unions are outlawed, and standards for pollution control and worker safety are nonexistent. Moreover, much of the capital that flows to Korea and other nations is American, West European, and Japanese capital. Korean industrialists, whether they work on consignment from foreign firms or whether they simply manage firms that are owned by U.S. or Japanese companies, must always look over their shoulders at the prevailing wage scales in other areas of the world. These are the conditions whereby workers are "willing" to work for $.67 an hour.

The important point, however, is that neither capital nor wages flow to these areas as water might flow down a stream. They are directed by the policies and choices of many individuals. A well-functioning American educational system would help students to understand this process and it would also help them to reinterpret such practices in ways that did not remove from them the factors of deliberation and responsible action. Contrary to the Carnegie report, such an education might not always be good for business, at least as it is presently constituted.

What is most interesting and most disturbing about the Carnegie report, then, is that it is able to appropriate a criticism that has been made of American educational policy — that it has often been designed to prepare some students for lower-level, routine positions — and then deflect this criticism by legitimizing that very same policy on the international level. In other words, if it is now important for American schools to teach children how to think, then one must wonder about the proper task for Korean schools.

The tone set by the economic analysis of the Carnegie Task Force is unfortunate because the report contains many worthwhile pedagogical recommendations, ones that are similar to those in the Holmes report. However, because the Holmes Group avoids the kinds of problems mentioned above, it is easier to take their document seriously as a report about education. Unfortunately, because of the timing of the two reports and the fact that a number of the recommendations are similar, the two have been linked together in the public mind. Moreover, perhaps because of the political influence of the Carnegie Corporation, the members of the Holmes Group have not seemed inclined to discourage the association.

PROFESSIONAL TRAINING AND LIBERAL EDUCATION

In any case, the Holmes report will generate considerable controversy of its own. For example, one of the concerns about the Holmes report that will need to be addressed is the effect it will have on institutions that are not research universities. I am especially concerned about the fate of education programs in the smaller liberal arts colleges, some of which already serve as centers of instructional excellence. Although graduates of these colleges would be allowed to enter teaching on a temporary basis as Instructors and could, of course, enter graduate programs to prepare to become Professional Teachers, there would be no special incentive to take courses in education since the rank of Instructor would be open to anyone with a liberal arts degree. Since some of the education programs in these colleges have been especially imaginative and creative, a program aimed at improving the standards of the profession should be cautious about taking any steps that could seriously weaken them.

Nevertheless, there are a number of good arguments that can be used to support the spirit of the Holmes proposal. A liberal education should provide the foundation, although not serve as a substitute, for the professional education of teachers. To advance these arguments it is useful to make a distinction between liberal and professional studies. Liberal studies are intended to provide many of the skills that a person requires to become an intelligent participant in public discussions while professional studies aim to provide the theoretical knowledge required for participation in a market through the development of higher-level skills. If one of the essential functions of a university is to maintain and improve the quality of public participation, then the Holmes Group recommendation that a liberal arts major be required makes sense not only for future teachers, but for any student seeking a professional university degree.

Consider, for example, the vocational pressure that the recent growth of business and engineering programs on the undergraduate level has placed on the undergraduate curriculum. If there is one lesson universities could learn from the recent tragedy of the space shuttle it is that we need to worry as much about the poorly educated engineer or manager as we do about the poorly trained one. While the latter may not be able to spot a dangerous flaw in the rocket, the former continues to manufacture the rocket after the flaw has been noticed. Thus, in insisting on a strong, liberal basis for teacher education, the Holmes Group has addressed an important area for undergraduate professional education in general. A professionally trained person is not necessarily synonymous with a well-educated one. In this respect, the

Holmes Group is on the right track. A university has a responsibility to ask more of its professional school students than it presently does. Having said this, however, there still are some questions that will need to be answered about the practical workings of the Holmes proposal before a full appraisal can be made.

First, consider the Holmes Group requirement that teachers be restricted to instructing only in those areas in which they have a liberal arts major or minor. It is important that teachers be competent in their subject matter areas. This is the only way in which the teacher can help students guard against the slanted presentations that often appear in textbooks. For example, a few years ago I was reading my daughter's history textbook. It presented the Vietnam war as a well-intended attempt on the part of our national leaders to save democracy in Vietnam, an attempt that was flawed only by the distance of Vietnam from the United States and the lack of a democratic tradition among its population. Good history teachers should help students to develop alternative interpretations. However, in order to do so, they would need to know much about their subject. In this instance, a teacher would need to know about the efforts of the United States to halt a scheduled election between North and South Vietnam in the 1950s as well as about the undemocratic character of the various regimes that were able to obtain the support of the American government. The teacher would also need to know something about the activity leading up to the Gulf of Tonkin Resolution and the treatment of Vietnamese villagers by the "pacification" movement. If Professional Teachers are to teach students how to question the received point of view, they will need to be able to exert judgment on the texts that are used in the classroom. The Holmes report is certainly correct in arguing that more than a narrow technical training is required for the Professional Teacher.

Nevertheless, the report is unclear about how its proposal to restrict a teacher's field of instruction to his or her major and minor fields is to be translated on the primary level of instruction. The implication of this proposal would seem to be that the self-contained classroom will need to be abandoned even in the primary grades. Yet given the nurturing function of the school, especially on the primary level, and the problem that many children might have in moving from the personal environment of the home to a more functional, subject-centered school environment, one must wonder about the appropriateness of this proposal on the primary level. The Holmes Group seems to recognize this problem because its recommendation for primary school teachers does differ somewhat from its proposal for secondary teachers. However, its recommendation that these teachers have the equivalent of a minor in each of the subjects they will teach is not a satisfactory solution. It entails too much material and too little depth. One suspects that if the education of primary school teachers is to be addressed in a satisfactory way some of the traditional distinctions between education courses and liberal arts courses will have to be reexamined.

Moreover, restricting teachers to instructing only in their subject matter major seems to inhibit the establishment of experimental, interdisciplinary programs by reinforcing departmental boundaries and legitimizing the view that the lines between subject matter areas are fixed by some unbending law of nature. Thus caution is needed in order to avoid one of the more subtle yet persistent problems in schools — the sense of fragmentation and intellectual isolation that a strongly compartmentalized curriculum often develops.

PROFESSIONAL HIERARCHY

A second concern is the Holmes report recommendation that the teaching profession be divided into a three-tiered structure. The initial rank of Instructor will not carry tenure and the license will be restricted to a five-year, nonrenewable term. The other two ranks, those of Professional Teacher and Career Professional, carry permanent tenure, with the latter having significant responsibility. Some will find this ranking objectionable because of the elitism that it seems to reflect. They will perceive this arrangement to be similar to proposals for merit pay and will be concerned that it will introduce a divisive element into the schools. While I believe that their concerns are quite warranted with respect to merit pay, the principle behind this proposal — functional differentiation and rewards — is in fact more defensible. Indeed, one of the weaknesses of merit pay proposals is that by allowing an administrative staff to make judgments about quality, professional decisions are located outside of the teaching profession. The proposal offered by the Holmes Group is different in that it offers differential rewards for differential functions.

One of the factors that makes the proposal unique is the implied relationship between the Instructor rank, which requires some supervision, and the rank of the Career Professional, which carries with it supervisory responsibilities. The provision for including as a part of the teaching force a nontenurable rank occupied by a temporary staff for no more than five years provides a way for the profession to control market factors during periods of both rapidly advancing enrollments and rapidly declining ones. Hence it adds a degree of stability to the profession that has been absent in recent years. If the proposal were to work, schools could meet the need for more instruction without oversaturating the market with more tenured teachers.

The provision for establishing a rank with considerable supervisory authority, including the supervision of instructors, and schoolwide responsibility adds credibility to the claims to professional status made by teachers. The important thing about the role of the Career Professional is that it makes a statement about the kind of knowledge base that is needed to support the profession of teaching. The fact that there is to be pedagogical specialization within this rank, as the Holmes Group suggests, is a statement that the body of knowledge required for teaching is too large for any single individual to be expected to learn in a relatively short period of time. An indirect implication of this claim is that if accepted, it will require that market factors be controlled by professional concerns. However, the more direct implication is that many years of study and practice are required to develop the expertise that effective teaching demands and that much of this expertise must be developed outside of the practical, everyday work of the classroom. Hence both Professional Teacher and especially Career Professional status require graduate work.

The key question, then, is whether the proposal is likely to work to achieve both the market control and the professional status that the Holmes Group seeks. The question of supervision is key here because were Instructors allowed to practice on their own, it would be difficult to argue that teaching requires a level of knowledge and advanced training that cannot be acquired on the job. While it is clear that the Holmes Group believes some supervision will be required, the question of how much and for how long remains unaddressed. The report speaks of "beginning Instructors" licensed to teach under the direct supervision of a fully certified professional. It is not clear, however, whether "beginning" refers to an individual instructor who is just starting to teach or whether it refers to Instructors as a group who, because of their status, are always to be thought of as beginners. If the former were the case, then of course there would be a serious chink in the professional armor since it would be difficult to find an acceptable reason to dismiss people who, having performed satisfactorily for five years, are not permitted to continue simply because they have entered the sixth year. While one might expect that during periods of teacher surplus, the six-year rule will be honored, it is less likely to hold during periods of shortage.

I have been told[2] that it is the intent of the Holmes Group to provide Instructors with continuous supervision over the five years of their non-renewable contract. Hence, even though the language is not clear in the report, the idea is that Instructors are really not fully qualified teachers who can work on their own. From the point of view of maintaining the integrity of the profession, this would seem to be the more prudent course of action. However, there are still problems with the proposal. After all, if a school can afford to supervise an Instructor for five years, and assuming, because of greater experience, that the amount of supervision required would be reduced each year, then would it not be more efficient to allow Instructors to stay on as long as they are needed rather than hire a new one at the end of the five-year rotation? The document is also unclear about the nature and extent of the supervision that will be required. If a great deal is required, then questions of efficiency will inevitably arise. If very little is required, then the claims for the legitimacy of the different professional ranks may itself be challenged on the basis of actual practice. I want to join the Holmes Group in arguing the need for a professional group of teachers, but I do find the problem raised above to be a difficult one to resolve.

PROFESSIONAL TRAINING PROGRAM

One of the more disappointing aspects of the Holmes Group report is the surprisingly limited treatment given to the professional components of a proposed teacher training program. While it would be unrealistic to expect a detailed course of study, one would expect more than the scant list provided. Indeed, other than the notion that teachers should be knowledgeable about at-risk populations, there is very little in the list of components that allows the reader to grasp the vision of the new, professional teacher that has guided the proposal's development. The proposal to develop demonstration sites is an attractive idea, but the Holmes Group has not really provided enough description of the work that would go on in them to warrant the likely expense. Indeed, many medical school training hospitals, on which these demonstration sites are modeled, are themselves becoming a serious financial burden and proposals have been made to sell them. Clearly, the value of such sites in developing professional attitudes and skills should not be dismissed, but I suspect that before a more expensive arrangement will be acceptable to the public, a clearer conception of its superior value will have to be developed.

Perhaps the most disappointing aspect of the Holmes Group proposal is its rather sketchy and narrow conception of the professional components of the curriculum. Its focus is almost exclusively on classroom practice. For example, it lists five required components: the academic study of teaching and schooling, knowledge of pedagogy of specific subject areas, skills and values implicit in classroom teaching, values and ethics of teaching, and clinical experience. Given the group's concern to develop teachers who are broadly educated, it is striking that there is nothing in this list that explicitly relates education to the context of the larger society. Of course it would be possible to interpret the academic study of teaching and schooling and the area of ethics broadly enough to include the social and philosophical context of education. Yet still missing is the understanding that schools are but one of the sites in which learning and education occur. It would be unfortunate if this aspect of many existing teacher education programs were to be neglected in future designs. If teachers are to be more than simply classroom technicians, they will need to develop the interpretive and normative skills required in order to understand the larger social context of their own work.

It is interesting in this regard to observe the changes that are occurring today in medical education. After decades in which most nonclinical and biological studies were excluded from the curriculum, many medical schools are beginning to see that it is necessary for physicians to understand the social context of their practice. Teacher education has long recognized the significance of this. It would be sadly ironical if teacher education, as it attempted to become accepted as a professional field, were to neglect this important area. While Professional Teachers certainly do need the skills required to effectively carry out their assigned tasks, they also need the ability to join the public debate about the tasks that are most appropriate for the schools to assume.

INFLUENCE

Because the Holmes Group represents but one constituency within education, the probable influence of its proposals is uncertain. One would expect, for example, that many smaller state universities that define their mission more in terms of undergraduate teaching than of graduate training and research will not greet the report enthusiastically.[3] Nevertheless, even assuming that most of the Holmes Group recommendations can be implemented, one still needs to ask whether we can expect an improvement in the quality of public education. To put it another way, can we assume that by improving the stability and status of the teaching profession, a corresponding improvement will result in the education of children in the public schools?

If the development of professional medical education is to serve as a model for teacher education, as many leaders in the profession wish, then the answer to this question is not obvious. After the publication of the Flexner Report on the improvement of medical education in 1910,[4] there was a significant improvement in the status and income of doctors. Moreover, there was a steady decline in infant mortality rates and an increase in longevity, which many attributed to the more rigorous standards of professional selection and training. Yet the connection between the increased status of the physician and the improvement in health was not as clear-cut as it seemed. Many advances were under way before Flexner's study was undertaken. Improved sanitation, diet, and immunization accounted for a good deal of the improvement that occurred. Moreover, the Flexner model has not proven to be universally benign. There are still many Third World countries where Western models of health care fail to address very basic problems. For example, we sometimes find countries where very large segments of the population die of amebic dysentery yet where the health sector spends its funds on highly technical medicine such as open-heart surgical units.

Increasing the stability and rewards of an occupational group by enhancing its professional status may help improve the services provided to a potential client population, but there are no guarantees. In order to get a sense of the possible effects on public school children of reforming teacher education, we need to take a closer look at the nature of the problem. When some of the recent reports on schools speak of a crisis in education, they are really referring to two related, but different problems. The first involves the perceived failure of the schools to produce the skilled people needed to develop and maintain the higher levels of technology in today's post-industrial society. The second involves correcting the high levels of illiteracy and stemming the tide of school dropouts. It is not at all clear that these problems require the same kind of solution. Nor is it clear that a teacher, trained to address the one, will be equally equipped to handle the other.

I am rather skeptical about the seriousness of the first of these problems, and have not been convinced that the difficulties experienced by our economy are related to the failure of schools.[5] Because this seems to be a minority opinion, some explanation is required. As I already mentioned, one of the problems with the Carnegie report is that it accepts the view that there is a direct and linear relationship between the quality of schooling and the strength of the economy. (*A Nation at Risk* also adds that a similar connection exists between the quality of schooling and the strength of the military.) The implication is that problems in the economy can be traced to problems in schools, and that problems in schools can be documented by the fact that standardized test scores have fallen over the last twenty years. Similarly, it is believed that the problem in the schools is caused by a decline in the quality of prospective teachers, who have consistently scored lower on college entrance examinations than students intending to enter other fields.

The Carnegie report continues this line of reasoning with an elaborate display of charts of the differences in test scores among different nations. Nevertheless, no convincing evidence is shown to support the link between test scores and economic growth or between test scores and a person's ability to teach. For example, the Carnegie report presents one chart that shows that out of fifteen countries, eighth-grade students in the United States score below students from all other countries except New Zealand and Sweden. The commentary alongside the chart tells us that "at a time when economic growth is increasingly dependent on mastery of science and technology, U.S. eighth graders' knowledge and understanding is below that of most of their counterparts in other industrialized countries" (p. 16). Yet given the countries listed above the United States, only one of them — Japan — has had a significantly more robust economy while those of many of the others have been decidedly more sluggish. If one were to take seriously the relationship between test scores and economic competition, then Israel should be a significant economic threat. For obvious reasons, however, Israel is not even listed on the chart. Education does have some relation to economic growth, but it is not a simple linear one, and in the present climate of international trade, those who are worried about economic growth would do better to look at such things as government investment policies and military budgets.

When it comes to the other perception of the crisis, the high illiteracy rate and the large number of dropouts, we see a situation where schools may have a more direct impact. Here, however, the implication of many reports that the intellectual quality of the teaching profession is inadequate to the task needs a very close examination. We simply do not know whether high SAT scores are indicative of good teachers. It may be that there is a strong correlation between doing well on tests and being a good teacher. It may also be that the relationship is other than linear. On the one hand, we might find that middle-level test scorers are too rule bound and therefore make only mediocre teachers. On the other hand, we might find that those who score high are impatient with slower learners and less able to detect the kinds of problems that they have in assimilating certain material. We might also find that the tests actually measure very few of the qualities required to deal with school dropouts or to handle problems of illiteracy. Indeed, in some areas where job prospects for high school graduates are slim, or where teenage pregnancy rates are high, the capacity to understand and articulate the concerns of the local community may be much more important than the skills that are measured by the SAT. Again, there is an analogy in medicine. By taking the highest test scorers, medical schools have chosen those students who are most likely to specialize in a highly technical area and have indirectly contributed to the decline in primary care and to the inequitable distribution of health services. The fact is that a lot of assumptions are being made about the relationship between test scores and teacher performance that have not been substantiated by research.

To its credit, the Holmes Group report has not rested its case on these assumptions. It has simply provided a sketch of the kind of knowledge that a Professional Teacher needs to have. Yet the question remains: How will this training improve the quality of education? I think there are two answers to the question. The first speaks to the classroom itself and the second speaks to the national system of education.

To expect a well-trained teacher to improve the inequities that exist in the educational system would be much like expecting a well-trained physician to improve the inequities that exist in health care. The distribution of health and educational services is a system problem and needs to be addressed on a system level. We expect a well-trained doctor to be able to diagnose accurately and treat well the illness that she or he encounters in the office. We should expect the well-trained teacher to be able to do the same with the ignorance that is encountered in the classroom. This is a minimum requirement, but it is an important one and speaks for better training programs than we now have.

Yet just as most of the conditions for health are found outside of the physician's office, many of the conditions for learning exist outside of the classroom. When these conditions do not allow good teaching to result in good learning, they must be addressed with the force of enlightened understanding. When these conditions are maintained by structures that are too powerful for a single individual to change, then a collective voice, with significant respect in the community, is required. A well-informed, skillfully trained teaching profession is a first step. However, as we can see from the frequent failure of the American Medical Association to support a progressive agenda, it is only a *first* step.

The actual influence of the Holmes Group report will not be known for some time. However, by opening up a new area for debate, by addressing the role of the liberal arts in teacher education, and by advocating a renewed vision of the teaching profession, it has performed an important service.

Notes

1   Henry M. Levin and Russell W. Rumberger, *The Educational Implications of Higher Technology* (Stanford: Institute for Research on Educational Finance and Governance, 1983); and Russell W. Rumberger, "The Growing Imbalance between Education and Work," *Phi Delta Kappan*, January 1984, pp. 342–50.

2   This point was clarified by Nancy S. Cole, who served on the group.

3   A similar conflict is presently under way in nursing education between four-year, university-based nursing programs and two- and three-year hospital-based programs.

4   Abraham Flexner, *Medical Education in the United States and Canada: A Report to the Carnegie Foundation for the Advancement of Teaching* (New York: Carnegie Foundation for the Advancement of Teaching, Bulletin no. 4, 1910).

5   See Walter Feinberg, "Fixing the Schools: The Ideological Turn," *Issues in Education* 3, no. 2 (Fall 1985): 113–38.

The Holmes Group Report:
A Teacher's Perspective

MARY HATWOOD FUTRELL
National Education Association

After agreeing with the Holmes Group on the need for professional autonomy and school structures that provide the opportunity for truly professional practice, Futrell expresses reservations about the proposals for differential staffing, the teaching doctorate, and the elimination of the undergraduate major in teacher education. She proposes a national teacher certification board cooperating with state boards to certify all teachers prior to their entry into practice.

The Holmes report, like the recent report from the Carnegie Forum on Education and the Economy, gives me hope for the future of my profession. The report is, as the authors acknowledge, "only a beginning"—but what a promising beginning it is. The efforts of the Holmes Group offer compelling evidence that responsible groups are at long last beginning to understand that education will never significantly improve unless and until the teaching profession enjoys the same autonomy as other professions. Responsible voices are actively contending that teachers must be granted the authority and latitude necessary to practice their profession.

The latest round of blue-ribbon national reports on education aggressively and rightfully asserts that the empowerment of teachers—granting teachers control of the learning environment at the building level—is the essential prerequisite for meaningful education reform. This new wave of reports reflects an emerging consensus among many public policymakers, a consensus that holds that higher-order cognitive skills cannot be taught by adhering to multiple-choice testing of lower-order skills; that modern education requires teachers with greater education; that politicians are not the appropriate persons to structure the teaching profession or its activities; that a political "quick fix" invariably produces permanent problems; that the fastest way to demoralize professionals is to overregulate them; that teachers cannot hope to prepare students for the information age if they themselves are condemned to organizational structures derived from the industrial age.

People are now realizing that teachers, like doctors, lawyers, and actuaries, are capable and worthy of professional self-governance; that those who have studied teaching — and the dynamics of learning — perform better in the classroom than people who bypass the professional certification route; that professional results will never be obtained consistently in the absence of professional compensation; that education — from prekindergarten through graduate school — is all one system whose parts must harmonize; that quality without equity is social injustice; that teachers and their representatives are not "the enemy," but rather the best, surest, and only hope for lasting improvement in our schools.

The Holmes report says all these things and more, and I am grateful. We teachers have been seeking professional status throughout our working lives. Over the last twenty-five years, we have continually struggled against the regimentation of our profession. We have sought to stem a rising tide of regulation that swept decision-making authority away from teachers and principals. We have maintained that the dilution of accreditation standards must never be tolerated. We have demanded tougher, more rigorous, more coherent teacher education programs. We have helped develop the research base that undergirds — or ought to undergird — the science and the artistry of teaching. We have worked to create a true profession.

The Holmes Group report is a welcome and powerful extension of these efforts. It too rests on the recognition that teachers need professional status and professional compensation, more and better preparation, more autonomy and less regulation, more collegiality and less bureaucracy.

The report takes the form of an extended *mea culpa*. The authors, deans of colleges of education at some of this nation's most prestigious universities, start from the premise that "our own professional schools are part of the problem" (p. 5). They chastise their home institutions for offering "many badly taught and often mindlessly required courses" (p. 5) as well as for delegating far too much teaching to graduate students. Admirable integrity, clear message: Improving K–12 education demands a radical change of attitude at the university level. Teacher education programs must no longer be the neglected stepchildren within the higher education community.

The Holmes Group moves from self-scrutiny to scrutiny of the schools in which graduates of education programs begin (and often swiftly abandon) their teaching careers. There, they confront a scenario that "embarrasses us as educators and as Americans" (p. 7): a profession under seige, one that is poorly esteemed and poorly compensated, overregulated and understaffed, short on professional development opportunities, lacking avenues for collegial exchange; a profession with massive responsibilities and modest rewards, a profession without power, a profession that offers its members a "noncareer."

What this analysis uncovers is the frustrating circularity that has thwarted so many reform efforts: Improving schools demands improving teacher education, but improved teacher education will make scant difference until schools improve — until, that is, teachers are "empowered to make principled judgments . . . on their students' behalf" (p. 28).

The Holmes Group sees clearly the implications of this circle of "mutual impairment": "As we try to improve . . . teacher education, we cannot avoid trying to improve the profession in which teachers will practice" (p. 6). This insight determines the long-range strategy to which the Holmes Group is committed. Yes, the group will push forward with efforts to transform teacher education, to catapult it into the twentieth century and into the center of university life. At the same time,

> we have become convinced that university officials and professors must join with schools, and with the teacher organizations and state and local school governments that shape the schools, to change the teaching profession. Schools no less than universities are places in which teachers learn. Unfortunately, that learning typically has been lonely, and catch-as-catch-can. . . . America's children need schools in which teachers can learn, in which teachers can thoughtfully investigate and improve professional practice. For schools in which most teachers can barely learn enough to survive are schools in which students will do no better. Together with other educators we have much to do, to make schools better places for teachers and students. (p. 5)

This message by itself justifies characterizing the Holmes report as an immensely valuable contribution to the reform debate. The report reflects the understanding that education is indivisible and that, as a result, solidarity within the entire education community is the essential prerequisite for lasting, effective reform.

Consistent with this understanding, the Holmes Group calls for a tighter alliance between education researchers and classroom practitioners. The authors maintain that the science of education promised by Dewey, Thorndike, and others at the turn of the century is now about to be fulfilled. Given advances in the behavioral sciences, there is today no reason why courses in pedagogy and cognitive development should not be as well defined, as coherent, and as substantive as courses in traditional content areas. The improvement of teaching, the report contends, requires greater emphasis on "pedagogical study requirements" (p. 53). Contrary to the views of well-intentioned but misguided reformers, subject matter knowledge alone is not adequate to the complexities of life in the classroom. The Holmes Group charges — justifiably, I believe — that disdain for pedagogy threatens to trivialize teaching (p. 29).

Despite my high regard for the Holmes Group report, I would be remiss if I were less than candid about my reservations. The authors themselves call it a "working document" subject to revision, and they have encouraged critical response from all quarters. In the spirit of collegiality, let me share my honest doubts.

I find myself uncomfortable with the report's career-ladder recommendation. To reach the top of this proposed ladder, a teacher would have to attain a doctoral degree (p. 13). This proposal is flawed. The doctorate is primarily a research degree, but K–12 teachers are not in the research business. A workable reward system begins by rewarding people for what they actually do, not for an irrelevant albeit impressive credential.

The authors' motivation here is understandable. They wish to extend to the K–12 realm a framework that has proved effective and is appropriate in the realm of higher education. These are, however, distinct domains. Rather than imposing a higher education standard on elementary and secondary education, I believe the group should concede that a viable compensation system for K–12 must develop from the realities of K–12 practice.

I also have my doubts about the proposal for "novice" teachers. The report advocates allowing up to 30 percent of a school's work force to consist of teachers who have not completed, or even started, a teacher preparation program (pp. 9–11). This proposal appears to contradict the group's own very persuasive argument that effective classroom practice demands practitioners who possess a firm grasp of learning theory and child development. The Holmes Group report would, I believe, have been stronger if the authors had remained consistent on this issue. My best guess is that they shifted gears in order to forge a proposal that would address current and projected teacher shortages. The members of the group would surely agree, however, that fully staffed schools are no guarantee of quality schools. To meet the emerging teacher shortage crisis successfully, we must raise the status of the profession so that it attracts high numbers of the highly qualified. To reduce standards at this juncture in the reform movement would be to signal retreat.

There are, in addition, ethical issues implicit in the proposal to use a large class of novices to generate an economic surplus that would support "upper-class" practitioners. Divisiveness would be inevitable. So, too, would cavalier attitudes: How, I wonder, can commitment to the profession be fortified by allowing one-third of the work force to consist of transients? All in all, I do not believe that the collegiality that the Holmes Group report so unreservedly affirms will be enhanced by stamping the teaching profession with a hierarchical structure. Nor do I believe that transforming the first five years of teaching into a Vista-like form of national service would increase commitment to the profession or improve the quality of instruction.

I am also concerned about the implications of combining the novice proposal with the career-ladder concept (pp. 36–41). It is no secret that there is a "resource ladder" in education. Resources flow to the "highest" educational level in an institution. In the case of the university, this level is the graduate program. In the case of a local school district, it is the secondary school. In all probability, if the Holmes novice model were adopted, novices would dominate teaching ranks at the elementary level. In view of current research that stresses the importance of having skilled veteran teachers in the early grades, this prospect is disturbing. To dilute the quality of instruction at the elementary level would be to fracture the educational foundation that has long been recognized as the critical determinant of students' future academic success.

Finally, I do not see how the goal of improving education is consistent with making it the employer of last resort for liberal arts graduates. Equally troublesome is the proposal to eliminate the undergraduate major in education (p. 16). What is arguably the most effective corps of teachers ever produced is now at work in our nation's elementary schools. These teachers are products of undergraduate education programs. I grant that these programs cry out for improvement, that they must be infused with a stronger, more comprehensive liberal arts component. But to dismantle these programs would represent the triumph of elitism over common sense.

The Holmes Group report fails to address the myriad difficulties that elimination of the undergraduate education major would generate. It is silent about the fate of faculty now employed in undergraduate education programs. It is silent about the economic effects on small colleges with large enrollments of education majors. And it is unconvincing on the issue of how this radical proposal would advance the cause of instructional excellence. Until the Holmes Group addresses these problems, the elimination of the undergraduate major must be regarded as ill-conceived and ill-advised.

My respect for the efforts of the Holmes Group compels me to suggest several counter-proposals. Instead of creating a class of novices with incomplete (or nonexistent) professional credentials, I would insist that *all* practitioners meet standards established by a national teacher certification board. This board—working cooperatively with state standards boards—would serve as the profession's conscience and would help ensure that all teachers are eminently qualified, never merely minimally competent. I would propose, as the Carnegie report recommends, that officials in every state declare a date beyond which they will not permit districts to employ unqualified teachers or to grant emergency certificates. Closing that back door to our schools is more important than decorating the front door with impressive sheepskin. That is why I cannot endorse the Holmes report recommendation to make the doctoral degree a prerequisite for attaining the top notches within the profession.

I do agree with the spirit of the report on this issue. Certainly all aspiring practitioners must know that they have to earn the privilege of serving in our nation's classrooms. They must know that they have to demonstrate mastery of the liberal arts curriculum and command of teaching methodology. They must know that they will be required to pass a demanding test developed by state standards boards (composed of teacher majorities) working in concert with teacher education institutions. And they must know that they will be evaluated regularly—and in accord with the most rigorous standards—during an extended practicum. This approach raises standards and status in the old-fashioned way — by mandating greater, more intense, more comprehensive preparation. The emphasis is on the skills that service in the classroom demands, not on credentials that establish an artificial and divisive hierarchy. I would have preferred to see the Holmes Group advocate a well-articulated and adequately financed system of career-long continuing education for all practitioners. A comprehensive career development program might have a higher education component, but it need not be degree-driven.

Looking at the Holmes report from a more general perspective, I see the need for a thoughtful and comprehensive statement on the mission of education. This report, like the spate of reports that preceded it, fails to offer a coherent vision of the purposes and goals our schools serve. It presents a philosophy that lacks an axiomatic basis. A more complete philosophy would, at least implicitly, suggest criteria by which to test proposed innovations and assess long-range reform initiatives.

Despite its overall excellence, I think the report is laden with contradictions. It seeks to purge the undergraduate education major at a time when the "products" of these programs constitute the most effective corps in practice. It calls for specialization in the high school even as it decries specialization at the university. It acknowledges the futility of "top-down" reform, but indirectly indulges in this practice by including only select universities among its membership. It affirms the ideal of empowering teachers, then excludes practicing teachers from its deliberations. The working assumption appears to be that not even one of several million practitioners is worthy (or capable) of playing a major role when the structure of their own profession is being debated. Certainly the excellence of the Holmes document would have been enhanced if practicing classroom teachers were numbered among the members of the Holmes Group.

These contradictions, however, strike me as evidence neither of insincerity nor of a self-serving mentality. Rather, they reflect the stubborn difficulty of the task the Holmes Group had the courage to tackle. For this reason, if for no other, the teaching profession owes the members of the Holmes Group its gratitude. The document they have produced may ultimately secure for teachers the professional status they deserve. The Holmes Group report has strengthened my faith in the potential inherent in this second wave of education reform. We may at last be on the brink of realizing the centuries-old dream of America's teachers: professional status, professional compensation, professional autonomy.

Facing Our Ignorance

PHILIP W. JACKSON
University of Chicago

Jackson argues that we know less about teaching than the Holmes Group report contends, that an engineering how-to-do-it view of teacher education is too narrow, and that the medical metaphor in education is seriously misleading. He proposes we turn instead to the tradition of teaching itself as the source for understanding this ennobling human activity and for designing our teacher education programs.

The Holmes report conveys the impression that we now know much more about teaching than we did a generation or two ago. I seriously doubt that claim. On the contrary, I have a hunch we may even know less today than we once did about how to teach and particularly about why teaching is so important for the future of our society. For the time being, however, I shall set that hunch aside in order to concentrate on what I take to be the report's unwarranted boasts about how far we have come and where we are today in our understanding of what teachers need to know about their work.

To witness this boastfulness we turn to the report itself. There we encounter its two forms — one explicit, the other implicit. The former consists of forthright assertions about how much is known. Examples are plentiful. One tells us that "scholarship and empirical research in education has matured, providing a solid base for an intellectually vital program of professional studies" (p. 50). Another reports that "dramatic strides have been made in the past two decades" greatly enlarging our current fund of "specialized professional knowledge" (p. 49). Still a third contends that "the promise of science of education [*sic*] is about to be fulfilled" (p. 52). There follows this elaboration: "Within the last twenty years . . . the science of education . . . has become more tangible: The behavioral sciences have been turned on the schools themselves, and not just in laboratory simulations. Studies of life in classrooms now make possible some convincing and counter-intuitive conclusions about schooling and pupil achievement" (p. 52).

Implicit claims about the status of pedagogical knowledge take the form of isolated words or phrases that sound impressive on first encounter, even though their meaning is not always clear. One example is the use of the term "knowledge base" to refer to the fund of verifiable knowledge now available to teachers. Another refers to "micro and macro mechanisms that make schooling possible" (p. 51). Additional examples include talk of "orchestrating the economy of the classroom" (p. 53) and of developing "a balanced portfolio of assessment approaches" (p. 14), the latter a circumlocution for a battery of tests.

The use of this kind of language contributes to the overall impression of there being quite a lot for teachers to know, much of it highly technical and quasi-scientific in form. The report underscores this judgment in its complaint about how little the job of teaching has been allowed to change over the years despite sweeping changes elsewhere. "Nearly all schoolteachers hold such creaky old jobs," the Holmes Group laments, "even now in the slick, high-tech years of the late twentieth century" (p. 7). Were they but given the chance, the remark leads us to infer, teachers who now hold those "creaky old jobs" presumably could advance to positions befitting the high-tech world in which we live.

But could they really? What are the pedagogical equivalents of micro chips and VCRs? Are there any? As soon as we pause to ask that question a larger one, lurking in the background, looms into view. Come to think of it, we suddenly ask ourselves, what justifies *any* of the epistemological claims the Holmes Group report contains? Unfortunately, the report is of little help in answering that question. Perhaps that is to be expected, given its brevity and the diversity of its intended audience. Readers accustomed to the documentation and detail of scholarly writing will find the lack of specificity frustrating all the same.

Toward the end of the report (p. 52) we come on the explication of a set of "powerful teaching strategies." These, we are told, include "maieutic methods, role playing, and social interaction and cooperation strategies," all of which are said to require "disciplined practice that typically exceeds even that offered by extraordinary teacher education programs." Here comes the specificity we have been waiting for, or so we might surmise. The examples that follow turn out to be disappointing. They are specific all right, but it is hard to understand why they are called "powerful teaching strategies."

They call on teachers to (1) "wait more than a few seconds for pupils to answer a question before filling the silence with elaborative comments that disrupt the students' thinking"; (2) "increase the higher order questions [they ask]," that is, questions calling for more than facts and other small bits of information; (3) "decrease the preponderance of teacher talk"; and (4) "provide advanced organizers," which means preparing students for lessons by telling them something of what is to come. The explication further calls for giving teachers "the cognitive resources to make pedagogical decisions and to manage productively the hundreds of distinct interactions they will have with pupils each day" (p. 52). What those resources might be is left to the reader's imagination.

The fact that the report fails to provide much backing for its claims does not make the latter false, of course. Still, it cannot help but arouse suspicions among the naturally wary, as we have said, and perhaps not among them

LIBRARY
OF
MOUNT ST. MARY'S
COLLEGE
EMMITSBURG, MARYLAND

alone. And well it should, in my opinion. Nothing I know of within the literature of research on teaching comes even close to justifying the epistemological claims the report sets forth.

This being so, I propose an editorial experiment. Let us mentally eliminate the parts of the report that I find offensive and see what happens. Let us suppose that dramatic strides in our knowledge of teaching have *not* been made within the past two decades, that scholarship and empirical research in education does *not* provide a solid base for an intellectually vital program of professional studies, that the promise of a science of education is *not* about to be fulfilled, and so on.

While we are at it, let us erase all expressions that conjure up images of laboratory manuals and college textbooks. Let us do away with talk of a knowledge base for teaching, for example, not because there is none but simply because the term sounds too cocky and confident. Let us also forget about micro and macro mechanisms that are said to make schooling possible. I have not the faintest idea of what they might be and I suspect no one else does either. Let us do the same with phrases like "orchestrating the economy of the classroom" and "a balanced portfolio of assessment approaches." Chances are no one knows what they mean either.

Having mentally blue-penciled the text, ridding it of what I call unwarranted boastfulness, we are ready to step back and assess the damages. Devoid of braggadocio, what remains of the report's rhetorical force? Does it lose its punch completely as a clarion call for the reform of teacher education?

I think not — or at least I think it *need* not. I see no reason why we should not proceed to upgrade the quality of teacher education in our nation much as the report says we should, even though we lack the kind of knowledge it claims we have. Indeed, I believe that by facing up to our ignorance we can only strengthen the impulse for reform that the report initiates.

Is that possible? Can we support the report's program while denouncing a lot of its rhetoric? To do so may sound contradictory, for it seems to imply that we can continue to educate teachers and even get better at it without knowing a lot about what works in classrooms. That apparent contradiction disappears, however, as soon as we break loose from the limited conception of pedagogical knowledge that has constrained the search for improved teaching methods throughout much of this century and continues to do so today. That same conception, I am convinced, underlies the epistemological outlook of the Holmes report. It explains why the authors of the report speak as they do about the promise of a science of education and much else.

What does that conception of pedagogical knowledge entail? This is hardly the occasion to spell it out in full, nor could I do so on my own if circumstances allowed. Therefore, the barest of remarks must suffice to sketch its basic features.

The key notion is the familiar one of cause and effect as understood in the physical sciences. The teacher's actions are conceived of as a set of causes leading to a corresponding set of effects, which are commonly spoken of as the outcomes of instruction. Usually the latter are couched in the language of educational objectives of one kind or another. Stripped of all complexity, the goal of educational research framed on this model seeks to tell teachers what they should do in order to achieve certain effects. The improvement of teaching, in this view, consists of establishing the linkages between teachers' actions (causes) on the one hand and student outcomes (effects) on the other. From this perspective, pedagogical knowledge boils down to knowledge of those linkages, plus whatever skill is necessary for the teacher to do what he or she must. The perspective is at once instrumental and utilitarian. The question it pictures as being uppermost in the teacher's mind is always: What will work?

There is nothing at all wrong with this perspective, so far as it goes. The important question is: Does it go far enough? Is it sufficient to embrace all we want teachers to know and to think about? Indeed, does it even come close? For me, the answer is unequivocally no. Had the authors of the Holmes report shared my conviction, I think they would have prepared a very different document.

The model of applied knowledge to which the report tacitly subscribes works quite well in some fields of endeavor but not in all. Medicine, for example, is one profession where it appears to fit, though less well perhaps than most laypersons imagine. Another is engineering. Both doctors and engineers have a rich fund of knowledge to draw on in their work. Innumerable facts and principles guide their actions, telling them what to do and how to do it practically every step of the way. Or so we commonly believe.

In law and the ministry however, another pair of venerated professions, the situation is quite different. Lawyers and ministers must certainly know a lot in order to perform their jobs well, but the linkage between what they know and how they put that knowledge to work is nowhere near as well defined as in either medicine or engineering.

Is teaching more like medicine or like law? Do teachers more closely resemble engineers or ministers? More important, to which model of a profession (if either) should they aspire? The Holmes report leaves no doubt where it stands on this issue. It wants teachers to be like doctors (no mention is made of engineers!) and the sooner the better, hence all the talk about the educational equivalent of teaching hospitals, "clinical pedagogical studies," "clinical faculty," and so on.

The comparison between pedagogy and medicine has intrigued some of our best thinkers from the Greeks forward. Doubtless it will continue to do so for centuries to come. In our own day analogies with medicine are the stock-in-trade of critics who want to upgrade the professional status of teachers. The comparison is obviously appealing, so much so that one day soon it may sufficiently impress federal and state legislators to make them come up with funds to support a few experimental schools based on a teaching hospital model. "Clinical" teachers engaged in "clinical" studies would then have a home to call their own. That seems to be what the authors of the Holmes report hope will happen.

I hope not. While wanting to see a lot more support for teacher education than we have today, I cannot help wondering why we must tie it to the promise of making teachers more and more like doctors. Can we do no better than that in our dreams of what teaching might become? Is our collective imagination so worn out that all we can come up with to impress the public or Congress or whomever is the overused image of a bunch of schoolteachers masquerading as interns?

Here my own cynical imagination takes over. I picture these teacher/clinicians moving about their classrooms, reading the chart at the foot of each desk, listening for the faltering heartbeat of knowledge aborning. Diagnosing, prescribing, prognosticating. See them bending low beside each pupil, dispensing bromides from their little black bags of pedagogical tricks. Clinicians, indeed! More like a cheap adolescent fantasy, I would say.

Those who point to the medical profession as a standard for teachers to emulate doubtless think they are doing teachers a good turn by making the comparison. Here is an enviable goal to which teachers might well aspire, they probably reason. What they fail to realize is that the comparison is ultimately degrading to teachers. It is so not only because the goal is so ridiculously out of reach in social and economic terms as to be almost cruel in the making but also because the analogy fails to consider all that is unique and ennobling about the teacher's work. More than that, either a medical or an engineering paradigm applied to teaching typically goes hand in hand with an emphasis on narrowly defined methods and techniques. What ultimately emerges is a vision of teaching that is almost exclusively technological in its orientation.

What alternatives are available? They are legion. Nor need we turn to other human endeavors, like the practice of law or the ministry, to find them. They lie within teaching itself. We uncover them as we consider the actions of model teachers, living and dead. We learn of them as we study the writings of those who have sought to penetrate the mysteries of the educative process. We encounter them at firsthand, sometimes with a jolt, during those moments when our own performance as teachers or as teachers-to-be engenders a kind of self-awareness that was not there before.

If we searched within teaching itself for a conception of what the profession might become, abandoning forever our dreams of a science of education, could we come up with an exciting program of reform? I think we could. Would it look different from the one we find in the Holmes report? Again, I think the answer is yes.

One difference would surely be in both the magnitude and the content of the promises made; that much should be clear by now. Another would be in the emphasis given to qualities like thoughtfulness and commitment as characteristics of those who teach. The report refers to these as "desirable professional dispositions" but does not give them nearly the attention I think they deserve. A third would be the rejuvenation of what used to be called the foundations of education, particularly the historical and philosophical foundations, a portion of the curriculum of teacher education that currently suffers from benign neglect. The goal here would be to make available to all teachers the rich traditions of thought and practice that are legitimately theirs.

The Holmes report is right. It *is* time to do something about teacher education. Let us get rid of all the Mickey Mouse courses that have given the enterprise such a bad name. If that means abandoning the undergraduate major in education, which it probably does, so be it. Let us also stop kidding ourselves and the public at large about how much we have to tell teachers, even at the graduate level, about how to perform on the job. Teaching teachers is an important job. Why cheapen it with false advertising? That is a boost it does not need. Let's face it.

Reflections on *Tomorrow's Teachers*

BRUCE JOYCE
Booksend Laboratories, Eugene, Oregon

Reflecting on the other recent attempts at reform of teacher education, Bruce Joyce urges twelve-month employment for professionals, major changes in classroom teaching, a unified professional development school, a reconceptualization of professional knowledge, and a coordination of the teacher education and the liberal arts curricula.

My first reaction to *Tomorrow's Teacher* is emotional — it is great pleasure that the evolution of leadership in teacher education has reached the point where a group of forty prominent education deans representing eminent universities presents a report that calls for sweeping reform in teacher education and discusses in frank and sometimes pungent tones the present shortcomings of programs to prepare teachers. The specific substance of the report may be less important in the overall order of things than the fact that such committed leadership exists. It is a big change from the early 1960s, when so many schools of education were busily rejecting the Academic Reform Movement[1] and objecting because so much of its leadership had come from outside the teacher education community. It contrasts also with the late 1960s and early 1970s, when education faculties used so much energy fighting off the performance-based reformers, who came from *within* their ranks. The Bureau of Research induced the American Association of Colleges for Teacher Education (AACTE) at that time to sponsor a series of conferences to bring those ideas to their membership and the team of disseminators was accompanied at each conference by an administrative staff member who began each meeting with a disclaimer — an announcement that the organization endorsed neither the need for reform nor the avenues that were being put forth. Even as recently as two years ago a paper was published in the *Educational Researcher* calling for comprehensive reform of teacher education, covering, in fact, several of the issues dealt with in the report under discussion here. AACTE was invited to respond and, in substance, asserted that the suggested reforms were either already in place or were in the process of implementation.[2]

So, I find the acknowledgment of the need for reform to be a grand event and the apparent commitment of the sponsors even more wonderful, and am not inclined to search for nits to pick. Rather, I offer a few suggestions about how some of the points can be fleshed out into workable platforms for action, and I find myself thinking about how the obstacles to reform can be overcome. One of the major problems in teacher education is that it was not designed with change in mind. Even widely agreed-upon areas for improvements, such as the need for articulation between academic courses and clinical experience, have been the focus of many plans for improvement that have had rough sledding in the implementation and have dropped by the wayside. No plan, however sensible, will accomplish much unless teacher education becomes a more congenial setting for innovation. Ultimately any platform for its improvement will have to present a plan for implementing the suggested reforms. Until the present only two types of reform have been relatively easy — those that have extended the period of preservice education (whole states have opted for fifth-year or five-year patterns) and those that have reified the proliferation of specialties.

Because innovation in teacher education has proved to be so difficult, reports like this one have to become a rallying point if they are to have effect. The style of the presentation is important if it is to be persuasive. I hope that future papers will be thoroughly documented and thus model the scholarly role of the major universities in the presentation of ideas. There is evidence about many of the positions that are taken and the lack of references leaves the ground unnecessarily unclear and some of the arguments less complete than they might be. Some relatively casual statements, such as the one asserting that elementary teaching is more lively than secondary teaching and that the difference is attributable to more extensive professional preparation for elementary teachers (p. 16), are not likely to be agreed on by all readers and the lack of reference in such cases weakens the document.

WORK TO BE DONE

The suggestion for a hierarchy of teacher levels or roles is an important one. However, I would like the group to deal with two related issues. The first is whether teachers at the top levels should continue to be hired part-time or should work full-time. I personally believe that a move to full, twelve-month employment is a necessary condition for professionalization, both internally for the profession and in the view of the public. The second is that hierarchy is the only type of differentiation that is mentioned in the document. There appears to be an assumption that classroom teaching will continue much as we know it. Contemporary technology and a quarter-century of interesting proposals for differentiating functions have laid the ground for the creation of schools in which the historic modalities of classroom teaching might actually become obsolete. It is extremely difficult to manage to think about the reform of teacher preparation and the professionalization of education without complicating matters by adding the need for major changes in the incorporation of technologies and the redeployment of personnel, but I think it has to be done. In fact, it may be that hierarchical differentiation will be much easier within a structure that differentiates functions as well. Also, the report gives little attention to the teaching functions that go beyond the classroom — the teacher as a member of a faculty, the creator, with colleagues, of the social climate of education, the builder of the school.

The revival of the idea of professional development schools is important also. It has historically been extraordinarily difficult to flesh out as an implementable idea. Ultimately such institutions might be the keys in the development of a professional ethos. The conception of professional knowledge will be pivotal in the development of such institutions. The sponsors of the report need to consider carefully how that knowledge will be framed. On page 62 they make a distinction among three elements of competent teaching: "subject matter knowledge, systematic knowledge of teaching, and reflective practical experience." Although the distinctions may be useful for certain aspects of analysis and the planning of programs, I believe that they need to be unified in the work place and that professional development schools should reflect the unity rather than the differences. Reflective teaching should not be separated from the consideration of formal knowledge about subject or teaching process.

The nature of professional knowledge needs major attention. I was a bit surprised by the assertions throughout that teaching technology is subject-specific. While much teaching necessarily deals with specific disciplines, a large reservoir of knowledge exists in cognitive and social psychology, behavioral systems theory, and other areas — knowledge that was not developed from subject-specific studies but that is applicable to the teaching of many disciplines. A major and serious effort needs to be made to define the current state of professional knowledge and to organize it in a form that can serve as the professional knowledge base of teacher education. As the knowledge base increases there have been some efforts to initiate a dialogue to assess and organize knowledge about teaching, curriculum, and school change and to identify the areas of professional functioning for which there is and is not a solid base.[3]

The organization as well as the substance of teacher education must be dealt with. The age-old problem of creating a coherent and systematic curriculum will not be solved by good intentions alone.

Finally, the liberal dimension of teacher education needs to be thought out anew. That teachers need to be well grounded in the arts and sciences and well prepared in the disciplines they teach will not be controversial. What is to be included and how will be a difficult question and one that has to be thrashed out by constituencies that are somewhat opinionated, to put it mildly. The committee serves little purpose in pointing out that arts and science courses are not always scintillating. Productive suggestions about substance and process would serve better to initiate a dialogue about the nature of substantive education for teachers. In addition, the social climate of the education of the intellect needs attention. The improvement of the profession involves the creation of a professional ethos in which substantive and clinical knowledge is respected and clinical practice conducted not by tradition or unreflected ideology, but in the serious mode of the best of the applied sciences. To create such an ethos requires a massive change in the social conditions of both the work place and teacher education, one that is mediated as much by the normative climate of teacher education as it is by its substance and organization.

A NOTE ON VALUES

The survival of democracy, the creation of a global social order, the navigation by individuals of a social world whose values are in flux and whose component of anomie chills the will and threatens the sense of self and social solidarity — these are realities as much as are the comforting verities of the three R's. We are not the first vocation to have to ask ourselves whether we should function as technicians or as moral social beings.

The ringing essay by George Counts, *Dare the Schools Build a New Social Order?*, is much on my mind these days.[4] Should our teachers shun the inner city work places for their own comfort? Should they see themselves as aloof from the national and global issues whose resolution will forecast the future of humankind? Should they be as driven to help students find themselves in this world as they are to help them learn to read and cipher? Should love, commitment to social improvement, concern for the aesthetics of life, be as much part of the fabric of teaching as the application of knowledge of the disciplines and the teaching process? The style of thinking of people like Maxine Greene would enhance the perspective of the report.

Can we create a conception of teaching and its preparation that blends the personal and the social with the substantive and the technical?

That we can, I think, is without question. But that we should, I believe, is beyond question. A reform movement in teacher education needs to be driven by the social value of the profession and the creation of a blend of the moral and the technical is the major work of those who would maintain sustained leadership.

Notes

1   J. Bruner, *The Process of Education* (Cambridge: Harvard University Press, 1960).

2   D. Emig, Commentary, *Educational Researcher*, April 1984.

3   For example, Michael Fullan, "Commentary"; G. Morine-Dershimer, "What Can We Learn from Thinking?"; B. Showers, "Skills Derived from Research on Teacher's Response to Training"; R. McNergney, "Commentary"; G. Hall, "Skills Derived from the Implementation of Innovations in Educations"; and B. Joyce, "Skills Derived from the Implementation of Theory-Driven Models of Curriculum and Teaching," all presented at the annual meeting of the American Educational Research Association, San Francisco, 1986.

4   George Counts, *Dare the Schools Build a New Social Order?* (New York: John Day, 1932).

Another View from Abroad

HARRY JUDGE
Oxford University

After viewing through British eyes the problematic state of American graduate schools of education in 1982, Harry Judge now sees in both Holmes and Carnegie the possibility for genuine reform. He argues that the funding of professional development centers and of chairs in the teaching of various school subjects should have high priority.

The current surge of teacher education reform in the United States (or, more precisely, of talk about it) epitomizes an international problem and opportunity. The problem is simple, but the opportunity at present inaccessible. Agitation about the state of public education, in many countries, has at last moved beyond the stage of proposing facile solutions to complex problems. Few, even of the ill-informed critics of educational performance, are now so naive as to suppose that anything much will be changed by a restatement of curricular guidelines, or by a toughening of procedures in assessment or examinations, or by getting nasty with teachers, or (most quaint of all) by a raising of the required standards of admission to the privileges of higher education.

The Holmes Group report is in part a symptom and in part a cause of a more realistic analysis. It is increasingly recognized that significant improvements in public schooling depend on an elevation of the standards of the teaching force (which cannot yet sensibly be called a profession), which in its turn depends on achieving a series of complex and interrelated changes in the ways in which the delivery of instruction is organized. This is why the problem is simple but the opportunity at present inaccessible.

What are those changes proposed, with varying degrees of explicitness, by the Holmes Group? First and foremost, the report has the wisdom and courage to recognize that—however urgent the need for reform within teacher education—fiddling about with its programs cannot of itself effect the necessary improvements. Simply to eliminate such programs from all undergraduate education, however desirable in principle, would be likely to make things even worse. Bad teachers are better than no teachers, or so at least makers of public policy would be likely to conclude, even if philosophers remain free to disagree.

It is, then, the nature of teaching and the distribution of teaching tasks and rewards that must first be changed. Only then can claims for any form of professional status be realistically sustained and (which is to say the same thing in a less refined register) only then can salaries and associated rewards be sufficiently competitive. Only when a significant number of prospective teachers can anticipate lifelong rewards comparable to those available to their contemporaries in other activities will a sufficient number of smart people wish to become teachers. Great Britain faces a crisis in teacher recruitment of unprecedented severity in 1987 simply because that elementary truth of the marketplace has been rashly ignored.

If sufficiently competitive rewards and satisfactions are to be offered, then it seems improbable that they can be offered to all those now calling themselves teachers. In the first place, there are altogether too many of them. The key therefore lies, or so the Holmes Group prudently concludes, in producing a nakedly hierarchical profession. My reading of the report suggests that this is a political rather than a logical conclusion, for nowhere can I find an ordered rationale explaining why or how *in principle* the tasks of teaching should fall into this pattern: There is not, for example, any suggestion that the distinctions may roughly correspond to those between doctors and nurses. This is just as well, since any clumsy hint of that kind would explode the fragile consensus that at present seems to embrace the teachers' unions in amity with the regulatory policy architects of the Carnegie tradition and the smiling deans of graduate schools of education. Before long, however, the contentious issue of how to define "a professional teacher" will break through the presently calm surface of debate.

I am nevertheless glad that the Holmes Group, being a realistic set of people, did not underline this question. They have been equally realistic, as well as ingenious, in squaring the circle of supply and demand. This is achieved by the device of Instructors — lively people for the most part, it appears, who having taken a bachelor's degree will plunge enthusiastically into teaching after a basic course in flotation, receive a license limited both in time and in scope, work under ill-defined supervision, and then face a choice. Either they make the necessary investment of time and dollars to secure a master's degree in teaching and become Professional Teachers, or they seek new pastures. Later, they face similar choices: go on to a doctor's degree (with a bit of foot-shuffling in the report at this point) and the status of Career Professional teacher, or remain in the mainstream category, or leave teaching. Such a pattern, if widely prevalent, might indeed produce relatively cheap and transient Instructors, and relatively expensive career people. But the problems bristle.

There are at least two ways in which superprofessional, professional, and subprofessional roles might be defined, distributed, and — the key — rewarded. There are problems with both. The first method presupposes a taxonomy of tasks: Who is being required or authorized to do what? The Holmes Group cannot be criticized, and least of all by someone like myself, for not choosing this method of definition. It contents itself, as it must, with serviceable generalizations along the autonomy-supervision continuum. If, however, these proposals are to acquire the weight they need and deserve, it becomes an urgent task of research and development to establish such taxonomies.

Inevitably, therefore, the Holmes Group is driven back *ad interim* into the second method, which is to equate the roles (Instructor, Professional Teacher, Career Professional teacher) with the mysticisms of academic status (bachelor, master, doctor). They have good reasons for doing just that. In the first place, it directs attention from our inability to generate other and more substantive equations. Second, it responds to the prejudice that professional status always has been and must be entwined with the *rites de passage* that the university regulates. Third, it brings business to the graduate schools of education — and especially the research universities — at a time when those establishments are more than usually uncertain about their purpose and anxious about their prospects.

All that is not only understandable but also, if it is thought important that the serious study of education should survive, virtuous. At the same time, it raises two related problems. There is a deceptively neat orthodoxy that asserts: Professions are distinguished by monopolizing a knowledge base; without that knowledge base the professional tasks cannot be discharged; the knowledge informs (or "undergirds" — a splendidly evasive piece of rhetoric) effective practice; it is generated and distributed by universities and especially in graduate study; teaching should be a profession; therefore the graduate schools of education within the research universities have (or will tomorrow) the knowledge base for teaching. The danger of such an orthodoxy is as obvious as the attraction. The danger is that, at several points, it may be demonstrably untrue. It is highly questionable when persuasively applied to established professions: law, the clergy, even medicine. The claims for the knowledge base must not, therefore, be overpressed. Power and autonomy, rather than knowledge, link the historic professions to the universities, and teachers should note that.

The Holmes Group is absolutely correct in insisting that the research universities must be closely associated with the formation of the teaching profession, but should recognize that in making such noises they are singing a hymn and not reciting a creed. In that way, the first problem raised by the claims of the research universities may be dissolved. The second problem proves to be more substantive, and relates to the graduate schools of education as they are. There are limits to both credibility and gullibility, and if able people are to make investments in graduate study then something substantial, as well as symbolic, must be offered them. Institutions providing such advanced study will need to change much more fundamentally than the Holmes Group, at least in its published report, acknowledges.

At present, or until very recently, such prestigious establishments distinguished themselves — for good external reasons — by neglecting teaching and teachers at the expense of other academic and professional pursuits related more or less peripherally to the diurnal business of the classroom. Changing that world, as the Holmes Group wishes it to be changed, implies a massive shift in objectives, in the criteria for esteem and promotion, in the balance of research, in the exercise of power. Given what the report so clearly says about the centrality of pedagogy, it follows that a new generation of specialists in the relevant fields must shortly rise to prominence. They are not yet in place. One test, ten years hence, of whether the Holmes agenda has "happened" will take the form of a study of faculty lists in selected institutions. If reform has bitten there will be fewer economists, sociologists, historians, administrative theorists (above all, them), and even psychologists, and many more specialists in curriculum, teaching, and teacher education. Where will they come from, and how soon?

One of the greatest of the many virtues of the report is its insistence on the concept of professional development centers. Integral to this insistence is the recognition of the indispensable contribution to be made to teacher education by the more able practicing teachers and of the importance of the proper articulation of clinical experience with graduate study at the university. There is even, as in the Carnegie report, *A Nation Prepared*, an unembarrassed and long overdue bow toward the analogy of the teaching hospital. The professional development centers are important in other ways as well, and not least as sites on which it will be possible to develop and analyze new patterns of schooling and teaching. They should serve to demonstrate both the viability of hierarchical models of organizing the teaching force and the concrete possibility of improving the working conditions and satisfactions of career teachers.

It follows that if I had the privilege of advising foundations and others on areas of strategic intervention to propel reforms common to both Holmes and Carnegie, I should propose only two. They would address the anxieties of the last two paragraphs and require the foundation of a number of professional development centers, and of a number of chairs in such areas as mathematics education, or science, or languages. These are things that could happen now. They have as much importance for the characteristically regulatory Carnegie formula, where the stress on an examination (and the neglect of universities) generates precisely the same problems of describing the knowledge base as the Holmes Group stress on the centrality of universities (and comparative neglect of examinations and national boards). The similarities are much more important than the differences.

Similarly, both Carnegie and Holmes raise dilemmas about undergraduate education and about minorities. "Teachers must have something to teach" has become a slogan, whether in Britain or the United States, that contrives to be both obvious and aggressive. On both sides of the Atlantic, its reiterated promulgation has led to an emphasis on subject studies, specifically but not exclusively for the benefit of future teachers. In the United States, it seems to be accepted by those who have the right to speak with authority that undergraduate education in the arts and sciences, and especially in the universities, is in a mess. What is less readily acknowledged is the structural difficulty of reform. It is one thing to argue that matters should be improved, standards raised, rigor cultivated, slackness eliminated, coherence pursued. To achieve these admirable objectives will not be easy within a culture of higher education that traditionally and justly prides itself on the virtues of accessibility, flexibility, variety, mobility, and so forth. The reform proposed would have the result, although hardly the intention, of increasing the volume of "failure" in the system. Will that prove acceptable?

A related dilemma is embedded in the intractable difficulties about minorities. The scale of the problem here is awesome. By the end of the century, one-third of all Americans will be members of a racial minority (and already in California there is a majority of minorities in the first three grades of schooling) and there seems little hope of producing a teaching force that will even begin to match this balance. Both reports (Holmes and Carnegie) confront this problem, but neither can find very much to say about it. It is, of course, even more of a problem for the examination-centered Carnegie proposal, which must stress such qualities as the objectivity and absolute nature of the battery of tests that will control entry into teaching. Here, as in the restructuring of undergraduate education, the problems are ideological or cultural rather than technical. Equity and social peace (as well as vaguer notions of democracy) do in both these areas conflict with standards, rigor, accountability, professionalism. Critics of the Holmes proposals, and even more critics of the Carnegie version, will not forget what happened to access to the profession for women and blacks after the Flexner reforms in medical education.

Europeans can feel only reverence for the noble ambitions for teacher education in the United States, and specifically for the proposals with which this special issue is concerned. Less ambitious and (I would argue) less imaginative societies have accepted, and are accepting, dual patterns of teacher education: a high-grade one for high school teachers, and a cheaper version for elementary teachers, or (more offensive yet) a university-based education for teachers of academic children in secondary schools, and something less for the rest. The Holmes Group, firmly rooted in the American tradition, seeks to establish divisiveness of a less unacceptable kind — one based on professional skills and commitments. Will it work?

The resistance groups reserve great powers of veto. Within the teacher-education establishment in its present anarchic and sprawling condition, there will be much opposition from those who see their institutional interests threatened by the imperialism of the graduate schools of education, which (they will feel) have taken little enough interest in the past in the teachers the "lesser" institutions have been allowed to produce. Politicians, and especially at state level, will be apprehensive both about costs and about the threat to their freedom to maneuver their way through cycles of teacher glut and shortage. Teachers themselves will show pathological ambivalence about whether they wish to use their collective power to change fundamentally the realities of teaching, with all the implications for bargaining and exerting influence. Simple-minded polemicists will continue to peddle solutions that look cheaper and simpler since they require only that teachers should be kicked harder. Parents and school board members will not readily surrender the control they now have, or believe they have, over "their" schools, in order to concede to professional teachers that autonomy which is a necessary precondition of serious educational improvement.

Still, there are two grounds for optimism. Of course, Holmes will not "happen." The United States is too large a country for any one thing to happen in it, and should rejoice in that good fortune. But where coalitions can be built, locally and regionally, effective change in the spirit of Holmes will be enabled. Not easily, for such change needs to be holistic: The rules of licensing, the structure of schools, the rewards of professionalism, and the functions of schools of education will all have to change in step with one another. The second reason for optimism lies in the very nature of the Holmes Group itself. It represents a coalition of those who wish to see change in a well-defined direction, without specifying with precision the legal and organizational forms that such change might take. There is, in my mind, no conflict between the Carnegie and Holmes proposals. If Carnegie "happens" — which must mean initially no less and no more than the successful creation of a national board and the manufacture of new examinations — then the work of Holmes will be greatly facilitated. But if Carnegie, which is much more of a high-risk/one-big-push enterprise, is defeated by the forces of darkness, then the Holmes program will remain in place. All that is required is that those leaders who have produced it remain together for long enough to protect and coordinate reforms generally acknowledged to be long overdue.

Teacher Leadership

ANN LIEBERMAN
University of Washington, Seattle

Exploring the relationship between research universities and schools, Lieberman asks us to think seriously about the real meaning of collaboration and of how real, not just credentialed, teacher leaders can be developed. She points out many things we have already found out about the characteristics and learning experiences that good teacher leaders have and how detached university faculties have been from the schools.

I would like to respond to two central thrusts of the Holmes Group report and the Report of the Carnegie Forum on Education and the Economy's Task Force on Teaching as a Profession. Both call for *teacher leadership* as a means of reforming the teaching profession and for some form of closer relations between schools and universities through *collaboration*. Although they are discussed here as separate thrusts, they are intimately linked. Working with school people is not the same as prescribing for them. One suggests participation, working together, and a linking of forces while the other suggests an aloof, all-knowing, imperious stance. Both reports call for the former, but the latter more accurately represents the past and present of the research university and its relationship to schools. Using the concept of teacher leadership as described in the reports, let us explore what additional knowledge and understandings might inform and begin to fill the apparent gap between the university and the schools.

A FAMILIAR ADAGE—THE MORE THINGS CHANGE, THE MORE THEY REMAIN THE SAME

We are beginning to gather some solid evidence that teacher leadership, knowledge, and skills are the result of a great deal of experience (only a small piece of which has to do with formal learning in an academic setting). An assumption of both reports is that there will be teacher leaders and that they will have advanced degrees, licenses, or something of the sort, to set them apart from Professional Teachers. Presumably they will not only be responsible for working with new teachers, but will provide a significant leadership function to experienced teachers as well.

How will these people be selected? How will they learn to be leaders? Who will teach them? What will they need to know or do to become leaders? Will there now be a credential in teacher leadership or a doctorate in it? One reading of the Holmes report might suggest that research universities could control who will become Career Professionals by providing the credentialing for such a position. Courses could be mounted, perhaps a "field-oriented" dissertation would be a requirement, so many years of teaching experience, working on a districtwide curriculum committee, and so forth. Maybe an action research project would be included. The university in this case would only need to justify the requirements and convince the states that such a requirement would indeed help "professionalize" teaching. Nothing would change in the university. Most professors would continue to do their own research, hold themselves aloof from what goes on in schools — and their administration would feel satisfied that they were participating in the reform of teacher education.

Similarly, in terms of collaboration, research universities could create "partnerships" with a group of school districts. School districts could justify the collaboration because they would be working with a "prestige university" and the university teams could say that they were working with school districts that represented a laboratory of the entire population of the state.

The university could offer lectures, courses, and workshops and the school people could come to them. Occasional conferences could have both university and school people on the rostrum. But is this any different from what we have had in the past?

THE CREATION OF TEACHER LEADERSHIP ROLES

In practice, teacher leadership roles of various kinds are already being created in urban and suburban schools alike. Opportunities to work with school districts and professional associations helping to create and understand these models are already available, although only a handful of people in the research universities are involved in these activities. What is important to our discussion here is to understand the questions that are already being raised and the knowledge that is already being produced and to ask why more people from research universities are not involved.

THE TEACHER SPECIALIST AS A CASE EXAMPLE

I use one such example to illustrate my point. The New York City Teacher Center Consortium (NYCTCC), under the leadership of Myrna Cooper of the United Federation of Teachers (UFT), has created a model of teacher leadership that is eight years old. It has already accrued an enormous amount of experience concerning teacher leadership in a large urban metropolis. Several interesting principles underlie this teacher leadership model.

The Problem of Selection

Specialists have been chosen for their jobs through nominations by teachers and principals in their own schools. Then they have been put through a screening process that includes interviews and simulations. As part of the process, the selection committee has looked for people who understand the teacher's perspective, a perspective that recognizes that teachers have many different styles and learn in many different ways; most importantly, that teachers are peers, not to be judged but rather involved in defining the kind of help they themselves need. It seems that those who become teacher leaders need not only good technical skills, but legitimacy from within their own ranks as well.

The Problem of Experience

Specialists have had experience working as teachers on several grade levels and as grade-level coordinators. They have had strong backgrounds in developing curriculum content. All have advanced degrees. Many have been active in community and political organizations and have very strong organizational skills. They also have strong human qualities — such as being good listeners, who are lively, positive, and outgoing.[1] Their experience has already differentiated them from those who have had more limited school experience. These people have also sought experiences outside of teaching that give them a broader view of their culture. Differentiated roles then means not just a different degree, or more years of teaching, but a broader view of the classroom, the school, and the society. Unlike medicine, perhaps those who stay in education but who seek and are chosen for other responsibilites develop qualities of leadership that may have nothing to do with a formal degree or a set of courses.

A Well-Developed Ideological Stance

Specialists are members of a cohort organized by the UFT. They have developed a strong ideological stance toward working in a nonjudgmental fashion. This does not mean that they do not take positions about good teaching, but that they take teachers where they are and work with them in a collaborative fashion to expose them to growth opportunities, research, and the best that is known about good teaching practice. They model professionalism by their own continuous inquiry, expanded repertoire, and high standards for what it means to be a teacher.

Strong Interpersonal Skills

Specialists have been studied as part of a larger group of assisters working in urban school improvement programs. Some significant findings include the fact that the key skills of people who play these roles turn out to be in the areas of social interaction. Effective assisters know how to build trust and rapport, are interpersonally effective, and generally work well with people.[2] Legitimating one's position in a school culture, often characterized by a bureaucratic rather than a professional orientation, turns out to be a key to the successful work of these leaders. They learn to weave their way around the culture, working well with principals while maintaining a strong teacher stance.

Context as a Critical Variable

The issue of context is critical. These people work in a large urban metropolis. Would it be the same in a rural school or a staid suburban setting? The need to adapt to the context and learn sensitivity to the particular culture — especially when one is attempting to change the status quo — makes demands on people that we are just beginning to understand. It appears that these roles cannot be divorced from the context within which they are created. These teacher leaders and their modes of working are as complex as the study of teaching itself. They learn through formal learning experiences, but their value orientation, their on-the-job experiences, their continued development encouraged by a growing sense of professionalism and success in helping their fellow colleagues, are critical. It follows then that if university people are to participate in this wave of reform, they must be involved in these contexts. Collaborative research, new ways of understanding professional practice, sustained involvement in cooperative working relations, experimentation — all need to be supported.

But are research universities really willing to examine their connection to professional practice? When Harry Judge wrote his book critiquing the research universities for their distance from "the field" four years ago, the response was to review it in the journals. Did anything really change?[3]

OTHER EXAMPLES

Successful models of teacher leadership are already being practiced in many places around the country. Early findings appear to show that these models are being created in school contexts, that they are heavily dominated by a "helping" stance, are part of helping to build a more professional climate in schools, are accepted by teachers, can be institutionalized, and can be collaboratively mounted by professional associations working with state and local school authorities. There are both full- and part-time models as well as teacher leaders in special education.[4] Where these differentiations of teacher role have failed, the reforms have blatantly ignored the importance of real, not symbolic, teacher involvement in the creation of policy, and in selection and implementation of models. Where the reform has led to competition rather than collaboration, it has engendered frustration and eventual failure.[5]

THE ROLE OF THE RESEARCH UNIVERSITY

What is the role of the research university in the study, understanding, or conceptualization of these roles? So far work done on either legitimating or creating ways to study professional practice has been slow in coming.

It is the rare research university that encourages its professors to spend their time describing professional practice and, even more rare, rewards them for such efforts. Being connected to professional practice, like teaching as an occupation, appears to be held in low esteem. Will research universities reward professors for spending their time "in the field" trying to understand these new roles? Will research universities encourage and be open to the growth of new methodologies that will encourage school people to become their own data collectors? Will research universities continue to define the researcher's problems as the only ones suitable for inquiry? (I once introduced a doctoral student to AERA as a means of expanding her horizons. After four days of sessions she remarked to me, "I believe that if all the schools in America sank in the Pacific Ocean, AERA members wouldn't even blink.") Will an article in *Educational Leadership* read by thousands of school people and teacher educators mean as much as an article in the *American Educational Research Journal*?

Collaborative study was once a part of at least one well-known research university. The Horace Mann–Lincoln Institute for School Experimentation at Teachers College was set up by Hollis Caswell to do collaborative research and experimentation for the improvement of elementary and secondary education. A group of professors worked with schools, developed curiculum, and organized teams of school people to work on *their definitions* of *their problems*. A wealth of literature emanated from this group.[6] We have at least one model that was very successful, in terms of both school improvements and the respected work of the researchers.

Can it be legitimated again? Will these reports give legitimacy and courage to the leadership of research universities to work differently with schools? Will at least some of the research community be encouraged to work with schools in real cooperative ventures? These questions can be answered only by bold initiatives that start at the top where the leadership encourages, rewards, and models a different kind of participation with public schools and where teacher educators are willing to participate, learn, and become sensitive to another culture quite different from their own.

If research universities continue to tell school people what to do without examining and improving their own institutions, the Holmes report will rightfully be critiqued for being "elitist." It will be seen as a rationalization for the university to "capture" future teacher education programs and new credentials for teacher leaders.

But it can also be viewed as a rare opportunity to reshape teacher education, to work on creating new roles, new structures, new methods of inquiry

—for both the schools and the university. My fear is that these reports may seem to many in the university a rationale for "doing business as usual." My hope is that they will stimulate new support for experimentation and leadership in the creation of real collaborative work between research universities and schools.

Notes

1   Lin A. Goodwin and Ann Lieberman, "Effective Assister Behavior: What They Brought and What They Learned" (paper delivered at the American Educational Research Association in Chicago, April 1984).

2   Matthew B. Miles, Ellen Saxl, and Ann Lieberman, "Key Skills of Educational 'Change Agents': An Empirical View" (submitted to *Curriculum Inquiry*, 1986).

3   Harry Judge, "American Graduate Schools of Education: A View from Abroad" (a monograph for Ford Foundation, New York, 1982).

4   A. Harry Passow and Ann Lieberman, *Special Educator Support Program Evaluation Report 1985–86* (New York: Teachers College, Columbia University, June 1986); and Judith Warren Little, Priscilla Galagaran, and Rudelle O'Neal, *Professional Development Roles and Relationships: Principles and Skills of "Advising"* (San Francisco: Far West Laboratory, November 1984).

5   Susan J. Rosenholtz, "Political Myths about Educational Reform," *Phi Delta Kappan* 66, no. 5 (January 1985): 349–55.

6   See, for example, Alice Miel, *Cooperative Procedures in Learning* (New York: Bureau of Publications, Teachers College, Columbia University, 1952); Stephen Corey, *Action Research to Improve School Practices* (New York: Teachers College, Columbia University, 1953); A. Harry Passow et al. *Training Curriculum Leaders for Cooperative Research* (New York: Bureau of Publications, Teachers College, 1955); Florence B. Stratemeyer, Hamden Forkner, and Margaret G. McKim, *Developing a Curriculum for Modern Living* (New York: Bureau of Publications, Teachers College, Columbia University, 1947); and Arthur T. Jersild, *Child Development and the Curriculum* (New York: Bureau of Publications, Teachers College, Columbia University, 1946).

Reforming Teacher Education, Rethinking Liberal Education

JANE ROLAND MARTIN

University of Massachusetts, Boston

Jane Roland Martin sees the call for a liberal education for teachers as a reflection of the Platonic tradition of emphasis on mind not head, thought not action, production not reproduction, reason not emotion, and asks what kind of education — both for teachers and for our young — does a society with our serious human problems need?

According to the Holmes Group, "the reform of undergraduate education toward greater coherence and dedication to the historic tenets of liberal education . . . is essential to improving teacher education" (p. 47). What exactly are those historic tenets? The report does not say, yet we would do well to understand them before we approve its proposals.

The historical roots of liberal education can be traced to Plato. Readers of the *Republic* will recall that in the perfect society of Plato's imagination there are three classes of people — artisans, warriors, and rulers — and that justice consists in each class performing its own job and no other.[1] Although every individual in the just state is suited by nature to carry out only one set of societal tasks and duties, education is necessary to ensure that a person's inborn talents and capabilities are fully developed. Since the well-being of the state depends particularly on the rulers' doing their job effectively, the guardian education is Plato's special concern.

Because Plato takes ruling to be a matter of knowing the Good, and considers this knowledge to be the most abstract kind there is, he requires the rulers of the just state to engage in rigorous theoretical study so as to perfect their deductive powers and develop the qualities of objectivity and emotional distance. To be sure, not one of Plato's guardians will be a "disembodied mind," for Plato believed that a strong mind requires a strong body. Nonetheless, he designed for his rulers an education of heads, not hands. Presumbly the artisans would serve as the guardians' hands. Moreover, considering the passions to be unruly and untrustworthy, Plato held up for the guardians an ideal of self-discipline and self-government in which reason keeps feeling and emotion under tight control.

In characterizing the kind of life teachers should lead as "a life of the mind" (p. 47), the Holmes Group implicitly embraces the ideal Plato held up for the guardians of the just state. Teachers, the report says, "must be reflective and thoughtful: persons who seek to understand so they may clarify for others, persons who can go to the heart of the matter" (p. 47). Plato's sentiments, precisely. Yet Plato would surely remind the Holmes Group that his educational philosophy is part of his overall social and political philosophy. He would, therefore, caution the Holmes Group that if it does not share his beliefs that some are born to rule and others to be ruled and that some are born to use their heads and others to use their hands, it must think twice about endorsing his educational recommendations. He would also remind the Holmes Group of the radical social programs Socrates and his comrades propose in book 5 of the *Republic*.

Concerned above all to ensure the unity of the state, yet perceiving private home, family, marriage, and child-rearing to be potentially divisive institutions, Plato's spokesman Socrates abolishes these for the guardian class. Thus, there is no need in the just state to prepare the guardians to live in families, be wives or husbands, rear children; their sole societal duty is to rule. What in my research I have been calling the reproductive processes of society — I define these broadly to include not simply conception and birth but rearing children to maturity, caring for the sick, feeding people, and so on — do not, of course, disappear from the just state. Except for conception and birth they are not, however, the guardians' responsibility. Hence the guardian education can safely ignore them.

From the standpoint of a society that perceives danger in the disintegration of the institutions of private home, family, marriage, child-rearing — one that comes close to endorsing Rousseau's dictum that "it is by means of the small fatherland which is the family that the heart attaches itself to the large one,"[2] if not his patriarchal imagery — Plato's theory of the guardian education must be considered incomplete. At a historical moment when child abuse and family violence are rampant, the failure of the guardian education to prepare people to carry out society's reproductive processes well must be counted a grave deficiency.

Ours is such a society and this is such a moment. But then, instead of attempting to move liberal education closer to its historic tenets, teacher educators should be concerned about the discrepancies between those tenets and both the ideals and realities of late-twentieth-century American society. Instead of recommending for prospective teachers an undergraduate program designed for people who will live their entire lives communally and whose everyday needs will be attended to by an artisan class,[3] they should be attempting to develop one that prepares students to carry on well the whole range of necessary societal processes. Instead of unreflectively endorsing an education that divorces not only head from hand and the productive[4] from the reproductive processes of society but also reason from feeling and emotion and self from other, they should be seeking ways to overcome the dualisms inherent in the historic tenets of liberal education.

Teacher preparation more, perhaps, than any other form of education should seek to avoid those dualisms. Correctly pointing out that teachers "play out" their values "in the ordinary interactions of daily classroom life" (p. 54), the Holmes Group does not consider the consequences for the hidden curriculum of schooling of an undergraduate teacher education designed along Platonic lines. Must we not expect that those who have been taught to lead a guardian's life will pass on to their pupils the guardian disdain for manual labor, ambivalence about practical action, and distrust of feeling and emotion? It is not only the hidden curriculum of schooling that we must worry about, however. Although Plato wanted his guardians to be so connected to one another that they would feel each other's pains and pleasures, the ideal of rational self-government he held up for them and the educational program he designed emphasized "inner" harmony at the expense of "outward" connection. An undergraduate program that conforms to the historic tenets of liberal education will therefore make it difficult, if not absolutely impossible, for teachers to make the kinds of connections to others one would hope to find in our schoolrooms and corridors.

In this regard it should be noted that the Holmes Group asserts that "teachers cannot be disinterested, lethargic, and uncaring" (p. 54). Unfortunately, however, the text does not make clear if the caring that teachers are to display is to be directed toward their pupils or just their subject matter. On completing their education, Plato's guardians are well connected to their own knowledge; it is their connection to one another, and to the artisans, that is problematic. Perhaps the Holmes Group's apparent unwillingness to speak directly to the issue of personal relationships is a reflection of the ideology of social atomism underlying the liberal education it espouses.[5] Whatever its source, however, a teacher education for the late twentieth-century United States ignores the three Cs of care, concern, and connection at the peril of all of us, indeed of the earth itself.

"While the determination of the origins, purpose and mechanisms of schooling are vital, the heart of the matter," says the Holmes Group, "is the structure of knowledge and what knowledge is of most worth" (p. 51). In invoking this familiar dictum of liberal educators in its discussion of teacher preparation, the Holmes Group commits the epistemological fallacy.[6] In relation to education, the structure and nature of knowledge does not have a privileged position. It can no more tell us what to teach teachers or how to order their curriculum than it can dictate to us the general outlines, let alone the specific details, of a liberal education. Epistemological issues are not irrelevant to teacher education. Our educational purposes and, ultimately, our moral, social, and political visions are the heart of the matter, however. To suppose otherwise is to ignore the fact that education is a human activity and that schools are social institutions. It is to forget that teachers are shapers not only of their students' knowledge but of their students' lives.

The epistemological fallacy represents a denial of human responsibility for educational decision making. Yet although we may be able to avoid the appearance of responsibility for the educational programs we design and develop by making them seem to flow from some abstract, impersonal entity such as knowledge, we are nevertheless responsible for them. It behooves those who call for an improved teacher education, therefore, to think as much about the shape their "products" will give to the lives of the next generation as about the nature of knowledge; as much about the kind of society they want the United States to be as about the life of the mind they want prospective teachers to lead; as much about the kind of world they want future generations of teachers and students to inhabit as about the cognitive competence of the teaching profession.

I hope it is clear that I am *not* suggesting that the Holmes Group turn its back on knowledge or substitute preparation in the three Cs for the preparation in the life of the mind it now proposes for teachers. In setting forth my reasons why a liberal education coherent with its historic tenets cannot serve as an adequate foundation on which to build a teacher education program in the late 1980s, I have been insisting that the Platonic dualisms be rejected. It must be understood that to embrace the neglected side of a dualism rather than the favored side is still to accept the dualism.

So that there is no misunderstanding, let me state categorically that, like the Holmes Group, I do urge reform. The project for teacher educators I am recommending, however, is neither so simplistic nor so impoverished as one that merely replaces an emphasis on head with one on hand, one on thought with one on action, one on reason with one on feeling and emotion, one on separation of the self with one on connection to others, one on the productive processes of society with one on its reproductive processes. It is a difficult project to carry out because it is possible to join together the two sides of the various Platonic dichotomies only if they are equally valued. The report of the Holmes Group bears witness to the fact that they are not. Perhaps, however, once we understand the historic roots of liberal education, we will begin to see the inappropriateness for prospective teachers today of the educational ideal Plato held up for the guardians of his just state and of the educational program he designed for them in light of it. And perhaps that realization will lead to the further one that the Platonic hierarchy of values embedded in liberal education both as we know it and as the Holmes Group would like it to be is ill-suited to a historic moment in which the fate of the earth and of all its inhabitants is uncertain.

Notes

1 A fuller presentation of the analysis of the *Republic* presented here can be found in Jane Roland Martin, *Reclaiming a Conversation: The Ideal of the Educated Woman* (New Haven: Yale University Press, 1985).

2   Jean Jacques Rousseau, *Emile* (New York: Basic Books, 1979), p. 363.

3   Interestingly enough, this is a fairly accurate description of the lives of many undergraduates today.

4   I define the productive processes of society broadly so as to include political and cultural as well as economic ones. See *Reclaiming a Conversation*; and Jane Roland Martin, "Excluding Women from the Educational Realm," *Harvard Educational Review* 52 (1982): 133–48.

5   For a discussion of this ideology see Jane Roland Martin, "Needed: A New Paradigm for Liberal Education," in *Philosophy and Education*, ed. Jonas F. Soltis (Chicago: University of Chicago Press, 1981), pp. 55–57.

6   Ibid., pp. 46–51.

Tomorrow's Teachers and Today's Schools

MARY ANNE RAYWID
Hofstra University

First considering the threat of the Holmes Group proposals to teacher educators in under-graduate colleges, Raywid then turns to criticize the differential staffing proposal as a cutting up of what should be a connected set of roles and tasks that all good teachers should be able to perform. She ends with a critical exploration of the idea of sound subject matter preparation for teachers.

The Holmes Group report, *Tomorrow's Teachers*, deserves to be read in at least two ways: as an entry in the excellence literature of the last three years, and as an action plan. Either way, it is the statement of a group with considerable stature, and sufficient clout to predict better-than-average chances for a somewhat fanciful plan for concentrating teacher preparation in the hands of a small proportion of the nation's universities.

The number of state and national groups working on the excellence challenge over the last several years has been estimated to be as high as three hundred. The spotlight focused first on the high school, was brought briefly to rest on higher education, and now shines in the direction of elementary schools. Certainly, however, the examination of higher education and its failings is not yet complete, and teacher education becomes a special case of that larger concern with the higher learning, as well as a prominent answer to what is wrong with elementary and secondary education. Much of the excellence discussion has consisted of the rhetoric of deploring, indicting, and in general distancing oneself from implication in the current situation. One finds echoes of this tradition in *Tomorrow's Teachers*, although this study is more temperate and reasonable in tone than are many of the excellence reports. That context is important, however, to a full understanding of the Holmes Group report, and relevant to judging its merits. New proposals are affected both by points scored by earlier efforts and by reports that follow. *Tomorrow's Teachers* is being extensively compared with the report of the Carnegie Forum on Education and the Economy's Task Force on Teaching as a Profession. The Carnegie report, with its more comprehensive concern, may come off the stronger. Its insistence that its recommendations cannot be adopted piecemeal, but must be implemented in their entirety if any are to succeed, is persuasive. And its forthright realism tends to point up short-comings in the Holmes Group report.

Yet there is much to recommend this report. With the beating that teachers have taken over the last several years, it is refreshing to see a serious, prospectively influential statement exploring their predicament and offering fuller, more accurate explanations for the conditions observers criticize. It is also good to read an articulate account of the complexity of teaching—and one appreciates the insistence that only interactive teaching is worthy of the name. The desire to connect colleges of education more closely with schools, and to improve the school as a workplace, is welcome and important. Throughout, the report abundantly reflects the broad historical and contemporary contextual considerations that have shaped today's challenges. It is also an effective means of promoting public awareness and understanding. One need not be an educator to be able to understand *Tomorrow's Teachers*. In all, one must see the Holmes Group report as a welcome addition to the national discussion of excellence and the determination to improve schools.

POLITICS AND GOVERANCE

As an action plan, however, the report has proved upsetting to a number of groups. It was prepared by officials of the nation's most prestigious universities, and officers of 123 such institutions have been invited to charter membership. Although the numbers are not large enough to be impressive—approximately 10 percent of the nation's teacher education institutions—the stature of the organizing group is. What is more, membership appears contingent on agreement to the Holmes Group proposal, and apparently carries a pledge to implement that proposal in one's own institution. Thus, the report must be taken seriously and its features and probable consequences explored carefully. In the space allotted me, I shall forgo any attempt at systematic exploration in the interests of a more penetrating look at particular features of the politics of the report—its prospects for school structure, including its differentiated staffing proposal—and aspects of its substantive recommendations for preparing teachers.

The Holmes Group report has generated some understandable resentments. It proposes that the business of preparing career teachers be restricted to major research universities. Temporary school personnel (Instructors) can be prepared by colleges and lesser universities, but only research universities ought to prepare the permanent teachers comprising the top two tiers of the suggested three-rung ladder. Equally threatening to the survival of a good many schools and colleges of education, teacher preparation should begin at the postbaccalaureate level. It is hardly surprising that the proposal has generated some steam. Whether better read as noblesse oblige or simply as self-serving, the suggestion that these institutions alone can do the job understandably raises hackles. (Nowhere does the report explain why only the doers of research are fit to prepare teachers. It is reasonable to insist that such a matter not be entrusted to those who fail to *read* research — but to insist that only researchers are fit for the teaching task seems quite another matter. It is not explained either how those same researchers, who largely abandoned teacher preparation by virtue of disinterest, are to be enticed into meeting the challenge.)

The resentments appear to extend beyond matters of pride and pocket-book, both individual and institutional. The Holmes Group threatens what have long been the nation's major policymaking organizations for teacher education. These are the American Association of Colleges for Teacher Education (AACTE), a membership organization enrolling more than two-thirds of the country's teacher education institutions, and the National Council for the Accreditation of Teacher Education, an accrediting body governed largely by AACTE and the National Education Association. The very existence of the Holmes Group as a standing body is a threat to the current power of AACTE. "It is the intention of The Holmes Group leadership," concludes the report, "that . . . participation in The Holmes Group eventually will serve as a quality check for research universities and their graduate professional schools or colleges of education" (p. 77). Presumably, one of the ways it will do so is by devising and administering "a series of Professional Teacher Examinations that provide a responsible basis for decisions on entry to the profession" (p. 65). Thus, the prospective impact and effects of the group and its proposals are far-reaching indeed, for the individuals and institutions and organizations primarily involved in teacher education.

SCHOOL STRUCTURE

Some of the ideas offered in the Holmes Group report are admittedly far from realization, and it is not quite clear just how things will go during the interregnum. Some institutions invited to become Holmes Group members are not currently engaged in teacher preparation at all. Their general research capacities are apparently to see them through the period of establishing a teacher education faculty and program and building the relationships with schools and school people that the report urges. Few suggestions are offered as to how even those research universities currently preparing teachers are going to increase their programs by five- or tenfold. The matter assumes some urgency, given that teacher shortages are already on us and the need for large numbers of additional teachers will become more urgent over the next decade.

It is hard to square such oversights with the report's emphasis on the importance of teachers and teacher preparation to school effectiveness. In this and other ways, *Tomorrow's Teachers* seems removed from what is happening in today's schools. To cite just one important example: Although the Holmes Group is willing to extensively rearrange the governance and conduct of teacher preparation in this country, it seems strangely reluctant to tackle the governance of schools. This stands as something of a gap in the report, since its overarching goal — "nothing less than the transformation of teaching from an occupation into a genuine profession" (p. ix) — certainly necessitates alterations in school governance structure. The report notes that making schools better places for teachers to work "will require less bureaucracy, more professional autonomy," (p. 4) but that is about the extent of governance discussion.

The Holmes Group does propose a three-tiered teaching staff, the second level of which wins classroom autonomy for itself, and the third level of which has earned the right to participate in policymaking for the school. This surely calls for modification of present school governance arrangements, but the issue is not addressed — unlike the Carnegie report, which quite forthrightly asserts that the control of professional decisions is necessary to a profession, and proceeds to consider implementation strategies. The result of the Holmes Group's treatment of this crucial question is unfortunate, because its proposals could well have the effect of increasing rather than decreasing present bureaucratic structures and controls. Despite some negative comments about bureaucracy, the report apparently accepts current structures and supplements them with yet another hierarchy of at least quasi-administrative officials. It does so by virtue of the functions it assigns to teachers at three stages of career development.

DIFFERENTIATED STAFFING

In some circles, the idea of differentiated staffing has now become almost as familiar as the idea of excellence. The plans for such systems are installed or under way in approximately forty states. In some — notably, Tennessee — "career-ladder" plans have already begun to falter. It seems unfortunate that the Holmes Group report reflects the central problem of so many of these plans: It assumes that teacher functions can viably be divided into pieces and that these pieces can be doled out to teachers as rewards, as individuals are found worthy of moving up to the next step. Thus, as I read the report, Instructors will have virtually no autonomy, and curricular and methodological decisions will be made for them; Professional Teachers will be permitted to run their own classrooms, but denied input to school policymaking; only Career Professionals will be both autonomous professionals and decision participants. The division manages the job of splitting up teacher-related functions into three distinct levels of role and status, but it does so at the cost of denying to the two lower levels functions essential to maximal performance! (From one perspective, then, one can view the suggestion as almost a caricature. It calls to mind Kurt Vonnegut's tale of enforcing equality by implanting beepers to interrupt the thoughts of the ablest every few seconds.)

There is now abundant evidence and testimony to the conclusion that externally controlled teaching practice is inferior to practice wherein teachers have the leeway to choose and adapt strategies to fit the circumstances. As Linda Darling-Hammond and Arthur Wise put it, research lends more support to "teacher behavior in which judgment plays a large role than to a view that presumes that specific teaching techniques or behaviors can be uniformly applied."[1] What this means is that the teacher who is carrying out orders, and who is not supposed to generate solutions and modify instructions, is teaching at a disadvantage, with a permanent lid on his or her effectiveness.

What is more, the evidence seems impressive that one critical key to teacher and school effectiveness lies in teachers' identification with the whole school, their assumption of ownership in and responsibility for the total school operation. It appears that the Holmes Group proposal would close off such engagement to all save the Career Professionals. To me this suggests a perpetuation of part of what ails us now — that is, structures that curtail and confine teachers' ability to succeed at their jobs and, not just incidentally, in so doing systematically serve to alienate them.

I have another problem, too, with the differentiated staffing proposal — related, but perhaps even more fundamental. It seems to me to put the eggs in the wrong basket. It assumes that only a relatively small proportion of the teaching force will be of top quality and casts its lot with nurturing that group and putting it in a position of influence and power vis-à-vis the rest.[2] Contrast this with the strategy Peters and Waterman found among the excellent corporations they examined. Rather than seeking and cultivating superstars, these organizations instead make the challenge that of eliciting extraordinary performance from ordinary people.[3] They seek, in other words, to maximize the performance of each individual. This is a matter of providing challenge, empowerment, and colleagueship. Contrast it with the strategy that would be directed primarily instead at containing incompetence — or making sure that the weak are controlled by the strong. It is the latter, somewhat defensive orientation that seems to me to undergird any differentiated staffing plan that seeks to close off segments of the effective teacher's role to groups of teachers. Such an arrangement might perpetuate a great deal of the coercion and dictation that undermine teacher performance now — changing only in the addition of a new set of controllers supplementing the old.

Lest this appear a paean to the equality of teachers, a bit more must be added. Certainly the Holmes Group is right in seeking to break in the tyro more gently than the customary total-responsibility immersion from the first day. There is also something to be said for trying to "unflatten" the career pattern of the teacher who stays to retire from the job. There may well be some differentiated responsibilities, and some differences in status, as well as the salary differences that are surely desirable, but we must figure out other ways to accomplish this than by closing off selected teaching functions to some teachers in order to award them to others. To provide help for the novice, experienced teachers might very desirably be asked to serve as mentors or guides. Their advice would surely prove more welcome, however, if the roles were not formalized into two classes of citizens, with yet another tier of superordinates and subordinates.

The challenge of variegating the career patterns of teachers might also be approached from a different perspective. For example, instead of seeking answers in the bureaucratic model, which places a premium on rising from one status to another (i.e., from one rung on a career ladder to the next), it might be well to explore how readily the professorial model might be adaptable to schools: Professors have considerable leeway in changing focus, orientation, even job description. They can readily obtain variety and novelty in their careers, quite apart from changes in their status and the assumption of quasi-administrative functions. Indeed, many professors would quite hotly debate the suggestion that a move to administrative work constitutes a move "upward" at all. Without suggesting that this is a solution — that is, that we move immediately to organizing schools as universities — perhaps this sort of model, and undoubtedly others, might be worth exploring before embracing a ladder model. Given the negatives tied to the proposals generated by the model, other possibilities appear at least worth investigating.

SUBJECT MATTER PREPARATION

The Holmes Group report gives much attention to the importance of sufficient subject matter background for teachers. I share that conviction, but am disappointed in the recommendations. At Hofstra, my institution, future secondary school teachers have always majored in the prospective teaching field, and for more than twenty years, future elementary school teachers have graduated with a liberal arts major as well as a major in education. I do not think either group is sufficiently prepared with respect to teaching content, and I worry about the Holmes Group's willingness to permit them to continue with very little more such preparation. The report suggests that the master's degree of the Professional Teacher would include "continued study in the . . . academic field," (p. 11) but since that degree program seems to be the sole locus of the individual's work in professional education, the academic field concentration could not desirably claim much attention. The doctoral study of the Career Professional apparently may not include work in an academic field at all. My criticism in this regard is not to outdo the Holmes Group's insistence on academic content but to suggest disappointment in their lack of venturesomeness with respect to this content and its nature. They do suggest the need to improve liberal arts education, but there is precious little about how to do it — or about the reasonable possibility that the nature of the prospective teacher's liberal arts concentration might well assume a form different from the major that is conventional for nonprospective teachers. Work in the liberal arts stands as part of the *professional* education of a prospective teacher. It is certainly plausible that it ought differ in nature from liberal arts courses designed as general education for other students. The question is not raised.

To cite another example, I remain unconvinced that a major in a liberal arts discipline is going to be of much help to elementary school teachers. I suspect they might benefit more from dividing the time involved among several fields they will be teaching.[4] Cross-disciplinary or interdisciplinary majors are certainly possibilities to explore. Similarly, maximally relevant academic preparation for teachers in many high schools might take a different form from the added disciplinary penetration that is the model for liberal arts study. I am not convinced that the pursuit of ever more advanced work in a field as sequential as math, or many of the natural sciences, well serves the professional function of a high school teacher. I am convinced that preparation for teaching in the specialty schools that the disadvantaged will surely require necessitates a *different* kind of subject matter preparation. Many of the most successful of these schools are thematically organized. Realistic preparation to teach in a magnet school with an environmental theme, for instance, might well include work in biology, zoology, botany, chemistry, ecology, animal husbandry, soil mechanics, political science, economics, and sociology. This sort of exposure might prove far more useful than a major in any one of these areas, but it calls for a different preparation from the conventional and would need to be considered carefully. Whether or not it proved to be a good idea, the point is that the Holmes Group seems to have simply made assumptions, and stopped well short of questioning what might desirably be scrutinized rather carefully. Under other circumstances, even such a fundamental omission might be subject to later consideration and amendment, but since this report is offered as an action plan and not just a proposal for discussion, omissions can prove permanent liabilities.

I conclude with the thought that taken as an entry in the excellence literature, the Holmes Group report is an important and provocative contribution with a number of messages that needed saying. Viewed as an action plan, however, it appears somewhat less successful, for despite its good intentions, it proposes arrangements that may not well serve its laudable goals, and it omits many that may be central to their realization. Moreover, it would terminate existing arrangements and machinery for substitutes that appear almost as problematic as what we have now.

Notes

1   Linda Darling-Hammond and Arthur Wise, "Beyond Standardization: State Standards and School Improvement," *Elementary School Journal* 85, no. 3 (January 1985): 328.

2   The report is a bit vague on numbers. It says that Career Professionals "could" be relatively few — perhaps 20 percent of the teaching force, that Professional Teachers "should" constitute a majority, but that "many would be" instructors.

3   Thomas J. Peters and Robert H. Waterman, Jr., *In Search of Excellence: Lessons from America's Best Run Companies* (New York: Harper & Row, 1982).

4   An appendix to the Holmes Group report recommends the equivalent of one major and four minors for prospective elementary schools teachers, but I am not convinced that this is a desirable or even a viable answer.

The Wrong Report at the Right Time

KEVIN RYAN
Boston University

Agreeing with the general aims of the Holmes Group, Ryan is critical of their lack of research and research findings to support their claims and proposals. He also sees serious problems with the idea of entrusting teacher education to research universities and their faculties, who have a very poor record of doing teacher education. He argues that we need reform, but not at all of the sort the Holmes Group proposes.

Trying to reform teacher education would test the mettle of a Sisyphus. Complaints against the way we prepare teachers are as constant as death and taxes. In this era of revived interest in schooling, teacher education has become a regular target for reformers and critics alike. And well it should. As a society we have tried to prepare teachers on-the-cheap for a high-demand, low-regard career.

It is no secret that of late we have attracted few of the academically gifted and energetically altruistic college graduates. Although there are heroic exceptions aplenty, American society is getting what it is paying for. If we are to maintain our position as a nation, however, let alone excel as a people, the brute fact is that we will need to overhaul our educational system. The first priority, the focal point of true reform, is the good teacher. Everyone acknowledges this: classroom teachers, business leaders, social commentators, and now a group composed largely of deans of colleges of education in large universities. Their report, *Tomorrow's Teachers*, has been the subject of rumor and controversy almost from inception of the Holmes Group some two years ago.

There is much to applaud in this report. It contains a sharp, though hardly fresh, critique of the career structure for teachers. It has resurrected from the educational limbo an excellent idea, the differentiated staff, and made it the centerpiece of its proposed reform. The report punctures the lame canards of those knee-jerk defenders of the liberal arts who make claims like, "The problem with secondary school teachers is that they have their heads filled with all that cotton candy educationese and they haven't had a chance to take real courses in the disciplines." This particular species of educational critic has been so inattentive to teacher education that it does not know that the war is over and the school of education lost. As the Holmes Group's report states, "Intending high school teachers in our universities thus take only two or three education courses. This has long been the rule" (p. 15). The report goes on to suggest that much of the drab, unimaginative, and mind-numbing instruction in secondary schools is a direct result of the uninspiring teaching future high school teachers receive in the liberal arts, which represents 80 percent or more of their course work. In general, the report's analysis of the problems is sound. Its solution, a restructured and presumably revitalized teacher force, is an attractive one. It is with the group's instrumental solution that I wish to raise a few questions.

Their solution, as I read the report, is to eliminate the undergraduate education major and replace it with what sounds like the two-year version of the Master of Arts in Teaching (MAT) Program, another idea that is hardly fresh, since the first such program in this country dates back to 1896. The group, however, is proposing the idea for both elementary and secondary teachers this time around. Before raising my questions, I feel compelled to make clear that I personally favor graduate teacher education. Also, I too believe that more is better: more general education, more academic training in the discipline or disciplines to be taught, and in pedagogy. We need to break out of the severe limitations of undergraduate teacher preparation. This current approach shortchanges the future teacher's command of knowledge and the general cultural context or his or her command of the theoretical dimensions and practical skills of instruction, or both. The constraints on time, just to mention one, are too great. Samuel Gompers's demand, "More!" is appropriately the demand of teacher educators. The feasibility of this proposed reform in the rough-and-tumble world of social choice is another matter, and the report does not help here.

What I find questionable about the Holmes Group recommendations is how unscientific, how unempirical their report is, particularly from a group allegedly representing the outstanding research institutions in education today. In a Jovian manner, they call for an end to undergraduate teacher education (I believe it is a measure of the group's political sensitivity that achievement of its goals would be a death sentence for a great many of the country's small liberal arts colleges, many of which would go out of existence without students coming to them to prepare as teachers) and then declare that the answer is to prepare teachers at the graduate level. How does the Holmes Group know this? Does the group have warranted knowledge not shared with the rest of the educational community? Are there several existence proofs to which these spokespersons for the leading research institutions can point both as supports for their claims and as models for the rest of the field to emulate? If the change the report is announcing becomes operational and then fails, the credibility of the field will be damaged for fifteen or twenty years or more.

What is the evidence that such programs will attract and hold large numbers of high-caliber students? What makes the members of the group believe that all these students and their parents will decide to pay tuition and living expenses for two years of graduate study for a low-paying salary? What about minority students who currently can barely afford a four-year program leading to a teaching degree and a job? The report does not appear to be research based, nor does it seem to reflect much hard thinking.

My second question has to do with motivation. Why are they doing this and why are they doing it now? Such a question is unfair to several of the institutions, which have a record of both doing teacher education and trying to add to the knowledge base in the field. However, the list contains many institutions that have used their undergraduate programs to build up full-time equivalencies (FTE) and to drain off resources earned for more prestigious doctoral programs. Serious preoccupation with the messy, clinical world of teacher education is left to the state universities and colleges.

Also on the list are the universities, among our most prestigious, that have had a truly contemptuous history of involvement with teacher education, institutions such as those that in the 1950s and 1960s took substantial amounts of money from the Ford Foundation on the understanding that they were making a serious and sustained commitment to teacher education. These same universities first denounced undergraduate teacher education and then, with much fanfare and self-congratulation, developed highly subsidized MAT programs. The clear understanding was that after the several years of foundation seed money dried up, the universities would continue their programs, but shortly after the final checks from the Ford Foundation arrived, in one elite university after another, these programs were abolished or pared down to closet-size operations in order to make work for the few clinical educators the institutions had tenured.

What has happened then? Have these institutions, like OPEC members, discovered their self-created glut of education doctorates and the flooded market of practicing teachers with after-hours, low-demand masters degrees? Is preservice, graduate teacher education the way to capture market share? Have their presidents and boards of trustees, noticing that American schools are falling apart, begun to ask them questions? It would be ungracious to dwell further on what appears to be the questionable motivation of some. Perhaps many of the new apostles of teacher education among the Holmes Group are simply coming late to religion. Still, other questions remain.

Can these deans of research institutions really change the character of their universities from professorial directed research to programmatic, school-based practice? Can they deliver their faculties? If they do, how effective will these autonomous, research-oriented faculty members be in the time- and energy-intensive arena of teacher education? Will they get religion, too? What evidence is there that the deans of colleges of education are going to be able to deliver to the trenches of teacher education professors from the colleges of arts and sciences? If there is a major university where this has been a widespread, sustained, successful phenomenon, it has been a well-kept secret, indeed.

Tomorrow's Teachers is clear in its categorical dismissal of undergraduate teacher education, but vague and incomplete in other aspects. For instance, why must all teacher education be at the graduate level? Why not start some pedagogical study during the undergraduate years? Child development? A career-exploration field experience? A philosophy of education course? More to the point, why does the Holmes Group not urge pre-education course work similar to pre-law and pre-med? In this way, the dedicated expertise of the teacher educators currently employed in the more than 1,400 colleges now preparing teachers will not simply be dismissed.

Few people deny that change is needed in teacher education. Pressure has been building up for something to be done. It is unfortunate that at the very moment when teacher education is in the limelight and has the attention of the policymakers and legislators, such a politically divisive and flawed plan has been advanced.

Tomorrow's Teachers

ALBERT SHANKER
American Federation of Teachers

Believing that arguments about the number of years of teacher education required and whether they are better done in graduate or undergraduate contexts are not important, Shanker accepts the basic model of teacher education found in the Holmes Group report, which includes a liberal education, mastery of a subject, professional specialization, and a structured clinical induction program. However, he warns that the impending teacher shortage may fill our teaching ranks with just any warm bodies unless we all work toward making this model a reality and instituting a profession-based national teacher exam.

It seems like only yesterday that the higher education community was united against the infidel at its gate clamoring that teacher education was unnecessary in the making of a teacher. The schools of education were certainly alarmed at the notion that there was no proven knowledge base in teaching and therefore no need for what they had to offer. Other faculty, gratified perhaps with the renewed attention to the importance of subject matter knowledge, were nonetheless sensitive to the prospect of losing one of higher education's arms and perhaps even being deprived of one of its whipping boys. Diverse though its comments, motivations, and convictions may have been, for a fleeting moment there was a united defense against the growing number of policymakers, education reformers, and citizens arrayed in battle against teacher education.

Today, that united front is engaged in internecine warfare over the Holmes report, *Tomorrow's Teachers*, and the closely related higher education recommendations of the Carnegie report, *A Nation Prepared: Teachers for the 21st Century*. All parties to the dispute agree that reforms in teacher education are necessary. Many even agree that reform of higher education in general, particularly as it relates to the preparation of teachers, is desirable. The blood is not being let over the nature of reform, which requires an analysis of the education problems reform efforts propose to ameliorate. It is instead being spilled over the number of years it takes to prepare a teacher. On one side are the proponents of the Holmes report, which calls for abolishing the undergraduate degree in education in favor of graduate-level training. Although the particulars of its plan vary, the Carnegie report essentially calls for the same. On the other side are the proponents of maintaining the undergraduate education major, albeit in a reformed state. Not to be forgotten is the camp whose position calls for the disappearance of teacher training from the academy altogether.

When this is viewed as a controversy over the number of years it takes to prepare a teacher, one's stance may just as well be determined by drawing a lot. There are four-year programs that do an excellent job and those that do a disgraceful job, both in the liberal arts and in education courses. The same can be said of graduate programs. There is, of course, no empirical evidence for the Holmes and Carnegie approaches, save in elements of past and present programs, and there is little evidence of "reformed" undergraduate education or of its results, save in scattered self-reports. What there is abundant evidence for is that the growing practice of issuing emergency credentials, which certify any warm body to teach, threatens to render debate over time-in-the-seat and degrees into the worst form of academic exercise. The footnotes may proliferate, but the infidels will have taken the ivory tower and the schoolhouse gate.

Forced to declare for the retention or abolition of the undergraduate education degree in the face of little or contradictory evidence in the academy and growing irresponsibility in the polity, I would choose to focus instead on the central contribution of the Holmes and Carnegie reports: a clear-headed analysis of the current context and problems of teaching and schooling on which to base a model of teacher preparation. The model both reports endorse involves a broad liberal arts education culminating in mastery of at least one subject area, professional specialization, and a structured, clinical induction program. One may be agnostic about the number of years it will take to fulfill the requirements of this model, but the model itself—the dominant one in other professions—compels support.

THE CONTEXT FOR REFORM OF TEACHER EDUCATION

Calls for the reform of teacher education are not new in American educational history, but they usually do not elicit interest from noneducators unless there is a well-publicized crisis in public education. This one is no exception. The reform of teacher education was not on the public agenda until public education became one of the top domestic policy concerns of the nation. The legitimacy—in some cases, the existence—of teacher education therefore will probably be a function of the contribution it will make to improving the quality of teaching and schooling.

Rightly or wrongly, then, the embattled state of teacher education is a direct result of the wave of reform that followed the discovery that public education in this nation was in serious trouble. Whether compared on curriculum, academic requirements, or student achievement, the performance of American schools, relative to those of other developed and even nondeveloped nations, was found deficient. The same verdict was pronounced when

American schools were examined in light of our own expectations, record of past performance, and the growing perception that educational achievement was vitally linked to economic competitiveness.

The ensuing education reform movement has already lasted four years and is still strong. Although the movement officially began with *A Nation at Risk*, a national report, most of the reform action has involved governors, legislators, and leading members of the business community at the state level. The results have been modest-to-substantial increases in education funding in exchange for tightened requirements for teachers and students, mostly through legislative regulation.

Tighter requirements for students in the form of more rigorous curricular, academic, and promotion standards were firmly in the tradition of most past reform movements. However, unlike earlier periods of reform, which hoped to succeed by creating a teacher-proof curriculum, the current wave emphasized the centrality of high-quality teachers. The ways it chose to do so were often perverse and destructive of the morale of the current teaching force, but the net effect was to force a long overdue examination of the nature and condition of the teaching force. The findings were shocking.

The existence of a steady supply of well-qualified teachers had become virtually a matter of faith in the United States. Certainly in the past two decades, to the extent that teacher supply was even an issue, it was in terms of surpluses and layoffs—a concern of teacher unions perhaps, but not of policymakers.

In the meantime, major trends were going unnoticed. First was the sharp drop in enrollment in teacher education, partially as a response to layoffs and, more significantly, as a result of the steady removal of educational and career barriers for women and minorities. Despite the purported attractiveness of teaching as a career—its "professionalism," "easy" schedule, "security," and "status"—the people who, next to teachers, knew most about the conditions of schooling and teachers knew better. Allowed the choice of nontraditional professions and occupations, the traditional talent pool for teaching began to reject teaching. The example was widely emulated by experienced teachers ready to take a risk for the prospect of decent salaries, working conditions, and professional growth opportunities. Over one-half of entering teachers do not complete their careers in teaching.

Had the leveling off of the school-age population continued as predicted, these developments might have gone unnoticed, but another set of trends turned the slackening interest in teaching into the beginnings of an educational crisis. An unpredicted baby boomlet sent the estimates for teacher demand soaring. Around the same time, it was estimated that approximately one-half of the nation's 2.2 million teachers will leave the field in the next six years. Replacements must come from the baby-bust college generation, a seller's market. It will take 23 percent of all college graduates in each of the next six years to maintain teaching ranks at the current staffing ratios, but surveys show that only 4–6 percent of undergraduates say they intend to become teachers. The unexpected return of former teachers and credentialed but inexperienced teachers may help, but the surge is likely to be small and short-lived.

Who, then, are the individuals who intend to enter teaching? There are still outstanding candidates, but the majority are in the bottom quartile of college students, according to standardized test scores. Many of them will be unable to pass the minimum competency tests implemented in many states to screen prospective teachers for basic literacy and arithmetical skills. In a number of states, over 35 percent of the prospective elementary-school teachers — all with proper education credentials — could not pass a multiple-choice, sixth-grade arithmetic test, even though the passing mark was only 65 percent. The current teaching force has been much maligned, but it represents the best and the brightest we are likely to see in education if present trends continue.

The nation thus faces a crisis of numbers and of quality in the teaching force, and at precisely the time when the proportion of students needing highly individualized, expert teaching is rising. Policymakers are moaning about the problem, about issues of equity and of economic renewal through education. The public expects results from the education reform dollars it has invested, and patience is not an American virtue. Expectations have been raised, and promises of higher standards have been made. And they are being routinely betrayed. In the midst of a reform wave that is predicated on raising standards, precisely the opposite is taking place; that is, "Labor Day Specials" and "warm bodies" are today being given license (figuratively and literally) to become the bulk of tomorrow's teachers. At the rate that unqualified individuals are being issued emergency certificates that entitle them to assume full responsibilities as teachers, the substandard certificate could soon become the standard.

The consequences for students will be devastating. The effect on able teachers will be demoralizing. They will certainly not tolerate the minute supervision that a corps of unqualified teachers will bring down on everyone's head, and they will leave. The message to bright college students considering teaching will be negative. They go to college to become something, and becoming something that anybody can become is not a mark of achievement. The teacher shortage will be overcome, but so too will the educational system.

AN ALTERNATIVE SCENARIO

The above scenario may appear overly dire, but it is a logical projection of current policy. Both the Holmes and Carnegie reports understand this and pose an alternative scenario: Instead of lowering standards, we should be raising them and so transform a crisis of numbers into an opportunity for higher levels of teaching quality. The condition that makes this possible — indeed, ethically imperative — is the development of a knowledge base in teaching. The initiative that would make this practicable — that is, maintaining reasonable, even improved, student-teacher ratios without resorting to unqualified teachers — is the restructuring of the schools and the teaching force.

Imagine, as Seymour Sarason invites us, a school in which the "egg crate" structure has been abolished, in which it is illegal to deliver instruction in the lock-step, factory mode to which we are habituated, and new arrangements permitting flexible class size and customized education become possible. Imagine, too, a school in which there are lots of adults performing valuable and necessary responsibilities in the schools, but the title and fully professionalized function of teacher is restricted to individuals who meet the requirements of the role. The choice between quantity and quality then becomes a false one.

The Holmes Group takes as its mission the education and training of the corps of professional career teachers that this alternative scenario entails. Although the model of professional preparation the report develops is the dominant one in other professions, it exists only in fragments in institutions currently training teachers. The Holmes Group institutions' efforts to install this model therefore will deserve close attention.

The first component of the model is a broad liberal arts education culminating in mastery of at least one discipline. Most high school teachers have fulfilled this component, but elementary-school teachers were generally exempt because of the view that they taught children, not subjects. A high price has been paid for this denigration of content and subject matter, and teacher education programs have been made to bear the blame.

To the extent that teacher education programs divorce pedagogy from content, the criticism is justifiable. The major responsibility for liberal arts and disciplinary education resides, however, with academic departments, and therein lies a problem that attacks on teacher education have obscured: the shocking failure rates of prospective teachers (and other college graduates) not on tests of pedagogy but on basic skills exams. The Holmes report's call for a careful examination of undergraduate education, both in and of itself and as it relates to the preparation of teachers, is therefore long overdue.

The second component of the model is professional specialization, that is, the systematic study of teaching and learning through rigorous academic and clinical experiences. The Holmes report is certainly tough on what all too often passes as professional teacher training. But where other critics of teacher education would dismantle the enterprise, the Holmes Group recognizes that the knowledge base exists to strengthen and elevate it. To institutionalize that knowledge base through programmatic means will be the greatest challenge facing teacher education, for without a demonstrable claim to a specialized knowledge base there can be no defensible claim to being a profession.

The third part of the model involves a structured and well-supervised clinical induction period. Unlike typical student teaching, this would provide a genuine laboratory experience with youngsters of diverse ability, motivation, and background. Novice teachers would not be forced to sink or swim on the job, as they currently must do, nor would they be compelled to abandon the lessons of their education and training to meet the exigencies of first practice. They would instead have the incentives, time, and help from experienced teachers to reflect on what they are seeing and doing, to internalize theory by subjecting it to the rigors of real life.

The Holmes report proposes the creation of professional development schools, the analogue of medical education's teaching hospitals, as the site for such induction experiences. It is hard to imagine the retooling of teacher education—indeed, the retooling of education—without such model schools. As Phil Schlechty has so wisely and frequently observed, a teacher's education and training occur largely in the schools—not colleges and universities, but the schools they practice in. And, as the experiences with the Master of Arts in Teaching (MAT) programs suggested, to train an exemplary teacher and then expect that teacher to survive, let alone grow and succeed, in a structure that mitigates against good practice is a losing gamble. We cannot afford such losses.

Professional development schools therefore complete the cycle. If a great part of the problem of attracting and retaining capable teachers is the nature of the school itself, then we cannot simply call for more and better education and training without creating the environments where the benefits of such preparation can be modeled and reaped.

The prospect of teacher education faculty, along with their colleagues throughout the academy, discussing approaches to implementing a new model of teacher preparation is an exciting one. The possibility of this discussion's degenerating into a debate about years, levels of degrees, and turf is not. The Holmes report outlines one sequence for the preparation of career teachers; there may be others. It is necessary also to give thought to the preparation of individuals who may not necessarily or initially want to commit themselves to becoming career teachers but who nonetheless are good prospects for the new roles schools must create to enable the professionalization of teaching and more customized education.

There will be, and ought to be, diverse approaches to implementing a new model of teacher education. That can be tolerated. What cannot any longer be tolerated is the contempt for standards. I am not much impressed by the rush of many teacher education programs to institute entrance and exit exams in response to the problem. Such self-referenced standards do not seem like much of an improvement over the present system, and I am uneasy about the implied shift from institutional to individual responsibility. It certainly does little or nothing to stop the Labor Day Specials.

The most sensible approach to reconciling diversity and standards is, in my judgment, to create a new, profession-based, national teacher exam, such as the one whose development is being funded by the Carnegie Corporation. If we have a sense of what teachers ought to know and be able to do, if we can construct assessments of this knowledge and ability in ways that capture the informed judgment and decisions involved in teaching, then there is certainly no excuse not to do what every other occupation at this stage has done: assert a national standard for assuming the responsibilities and prerogatives of professionals. That is not, nor should it be, the responsibility of teacher educators alone. It is the obligation of the teaching profession to itself, to its clients, and to the public.

The Holmes Group Report:
Its Latent Political Agenda

ALAN R. TOM
Washington University, St. Louis

As president of the Association of Independent Liberal Arts Colleges for Teacher Education, Alan Tom examines the Holmes Group proposal to eliminate the undergraduate teacher education major and sees more concern with the structure than the substance of reform and finds a deep commitment to a linear form of professional study. This, he contends, was the unconscious assertion by research-oriented universities of their own political interests.

The Holmes report is an apparently straightforward platform for the reform of teacher education. The major recommendations include eliminating undergraduate majors in education, moving professional preparation to the graduate level, improving the subject matter preparation of teachers, establishing a set of differentiated teaching roles, creating new institutional relationships between schools and universities, and a few other reforms the authors believe are integrally related to the five goals outlined in the report. While it is possible to argue with the logic connecting specific recommendations to these goals, especially the recommendations for mandating master's level teacher preparation and for conducting the professional aspect of that preparation in autonomous graduate schools of education,[1] I want to focus on two questions not directed toward the internal logic of the report.

These questions are designed to expose a latent political agenda in the Holmes proposals and to reveal critical reform issues omitted from the report. First, why is there such an uproar over the Holmes recommendations, many of which are old ideas? Second, what policies or institutional arrangements does the Holmes report take for granted? The latter question should help identify key omissions while the former should help lay bare political nerves touched by the report.

The uproar surrounding the Holmes report is surprising in that so many of the key recommendations have been put forward again and again, usually without great fanfare or dispute. For example, precursors to the professional development school idea are common, including such proposals as profes-

The author gratefully acknowledges Dan Liston, who made valuable comments on drafts of this article.

sional development centers, collaborative teaching centers, clinical schools modeled after teaching hospitals, and so forth.[2] Yet these interinstitutional arrangements, many of which have been implemented, were not as controversial as is the Holmes report. Other precursors could be cited, such as differentiated staffing,[3] or recommendations for upgrading the subject matter preparation of teachers.

We would have to go back to Conant's *The Education of American Teachers*[4] to find the degree of interest and controversy engendered by the Holmes report. How can we account for the current conflict and controversy[5] if so many of the recommendations are neither new nor widely debated? A significant clue occurs, I believe, in a letter to the editor of the *Chronicle of Higher Education* from the state superintendent of the Arizona Department of Education,[6] noting that the invited charter members of the Holmes Group prepare only about 20 percent of the nation's teachers; four-year private colleges and universities and the institutions belonging to the American Association of State Colleges and Universities that also educate teachers are not represented.

The omission of these institutions is not the sole cause of controversy, as the Holmes Group institutions indicated from the beginning that their focus was on how research-oriented institutions could improve their own programs. In an early funding proposal, the emphasis was not so much on excluding institutions from Holmes membership as on identifying and remedying "self-acknowledged problems." This proposal readily admitted that a major impediment to reforming the overall field of teacher education was "problems stemming from an apparent disdain for, or at least disinterest in, teacher education on the part of the leading research universities in the United States."[7] Thus, in 1984 Holmes Group institutions clearly assumed some responsibility for the national condition of teacher education and proclaimed their interest in improving their own programs. Moreover, as late as early 1986, Holmes Group leaders continued to stress the self-help theme and to emphasize that they had no desire to take over teacher education.[8]

Two months later, however, when the final report was issued, the Holmes Group Executive Board not only established goals and action commitments for their own programs but also attempted to define a differentiated role and certification structure applicable to all teacher education institutions. "The Holmes Group commits itself to the development of a differentiated structure at three levels: the Career Professional Teacher . . . the Professional Teacher . . . and the Instructor. . . . The Holmes Group also commits itself to make the changes in graduate education necessary to prepare professional teachers for this differentiated structure and *to use its influence to change state and local policy*" (p. 65; emphasis added). Thus if the Holmes institutions succeed in altering certification policy in the various states, the graduates of four-year institutions will qualify for nothing more than the Instructor role, a short-term role whose status is low.

The potential elimination of undergraduate teacher preparation has engendered varied responses. Some individuals believe Holmes institutions are trying to create a market for Holmes Group graduates or to eliminate the competition, while two teacher education groups representing primarily four-year programs have adopted policy statements defending the value and advantages of these programs.[9] There has also been favorable reaction to the Holmes proposal for eliminating undergraduate teacher education, but most of the negative reactions to the report have focused on the attempt of the Holmes Group to phase out four-year teacher preparation programs.

I have no reason to believe that the Holmes Group leadership consciously planned to push some institutions out of the professional preparation of teachers, even though many liberal arts colleges and some regional universities would have trouble mounting the postbaccalaureate professional preparation required by Holmes standards. Neither the published documents nor my personal observations as a member of the Holmes planning group (summer of 1985 to April 1986) suggest any "conspiracy" on the part of Holmes deans to eliminate certain institutions from engaging in teacher education. But the issue of the role of undergraduate teacher preparation was vigorously debated throughout the planning period, and was one point addressed by eight deans, myself included, who wanted the Holmes agenda to recognize the possibility of obtaining a teaching certificate through an improved four-year program.[10] In the end, the executive board rejected this possibility.

Whatever the rationale of the leadership, their decision to mandate graduate-level professional preparation has caused too much attention to be given to the structural changes advocated in the final report. In particular, those who think their programs threatened have reacted in defense of these programs. Increasingly the issue has become how long a program should be, not what its content ought to be. Henry W. Holmes, for whom the Holmes Group is named, warned against this way of construing the reform issue:

> The burning question . . . seems to me to be not the question now often debated among university teachers of Education: "Shall a Master's degree be required of prospective secondary-school teachers?" but rather the question: "How shall the work for the Master's degree that ought obviously to be required of most prospective secondary-school teachers be so conducted that those who attain it may carry into the schools technical competence that can keep itself alive, a professional philosophy that will endure and grow, and a cultural and scholarly foundation that will make them bearers of light to the youth they teach?"[11]

By focusing on structural changes involving level of degree and corresponding types of certification, the Holmes Group has diverted the national debate on teacher education reform to procedural rather than substantive issues.

Further light may be shed on why the debate is so focused on the length of programs if we ask our second question: What policies or institutional arrangements does the Holmes report take for granted? One such assumption seems to be that the issue of the professional curriculum is one that can wait until the structural reforms concerning degree level and types of certification are instituted. While there is discussion of the professional curriculum in the report, this discussion is brief and disconcertingly vague. For example, we are told that "teacher education long has been intellectually weak" (p. 6) and that the essence of reforming the professional education of teachers entails "identifying the knowledge base for competent teaching, and developing the content and strategies whereby it is imparted" (p. 49). Further, the report claims that a program of professional studies contains five components, and each component is briefly described. That is about as far as the analysis proceeds, as we are advised that the next step is for "university faculty, working with selected clinical faculty from cooperating schools . . . to reexamine contemporary pedagogical offerings" (p. 55).

For anyone who wants to address the substance of professional education, there are few concrete ideas to analyze. Sometime off in the future these substantive questions need to be confronted, but for now, the report suggests, it is enough to recognize that the current professional curriculum is weak and that this curriculum needs the infusion of a research-derived knowledge base. One wonders just where this knowledge base is, if it is not in the programs of the very institutions composing the Holmes Group. After all, these institutions, according to the preface of the report, have "the faculty who, on the whole, are the nation's best and most authoritative sources of information in their fields" (p. ix).

One can only speculate why the professional curriculum, including internship, is literally ignored in the Holmes report. One reason may be that redesigning this curriculum is a much more complicated issue than infusing research-based knowledge into the graduate studies of a teacher. Or it may be that the participating deans found that achieving consensus on such a complex issue as the content and strategies of the professional curriculum was extremely difficult. Both of these reasons seem plausible, but it seems equally difficult to agree on the desirability of a single structural model for preservice teacher preparation, and this latter task was completed. One must therefore surmise that reform of the degree and certification structures was a higher priority to Holmes Group deans than was reform of the content of the professional curriculum.

A second topic taken for granted is the policy that the preparation of Professional Teachers has to be completed before these teachers assume classroom responsibility.[12] One of the key commitments each Holmes institution must make is that it will not recommend for a professional certificate any person completing an undergraduate teacher education program, even if that student majors in an academic discipline and completes certification requirements. Such students can become Instructors, teachers working for several years under the close supervision of Career Professionals. The Professional Teacher must complete an academically oriented baccalaureate degree and then do graduate study—academic as well as pedagogical studies and internship—that results in a master's degree in teaching. The entire training investment occurs prior to classroom teaching, not only dramatically increasing preparation costs but also eliminating alternative routes to becoming a Professional Teacher. Rejected are such possibilities as achieving Professional Teacher status by (1) combining undergraduate teacher preparation with internship, even for skillful and talented prospective teachers, or (2) coordinating a postbaccalaureate internship with team-taught professional courses, followed by provisional certification, several years of teaching, and ultimately a subsidized sabbatical for those whose performance merits Professional Teacher status,[13] or (3) having undergraduate teacher education lead to several years of full-fledged teaching, after which there would be a full-time sabbatical year for study in one or more subject matter areas. The purpose of mentioning these possibilities is not so much to argue their superiority as to illustrate that alternatives do exist to the linear progression of academic study, professional study, and internship.

There is evidence that alternatives to the linear progression were entertained, even if only by a minority of Holmes Group deans,[14] but these discussions were brief, and the minority favoring the alternatives never articulated them very well. In a sense, all of these deans were unable to escape the professional school model in which preprofessional work is followed by professional studies, with clinical work coming at the end. This linear model of teacher preparation, perhaps because it fits so comfortably with the standard graduate school model of professional preparation, was never seriously questioned.

Looking back over what the Holmes Group took for granted (the linear model of professional school training and the supremacy of structure over content), as well as their attempt to eliminate undergraduate teacher preparation, I believe it fair to conclude that their proposals have a strong political dimension. In a sense, the proposals are an attempt by the research-oriented universities to assert their primacy in teacher education by rewriting its role and certification structure so that this structure better conforms to the way these institutions operate. This process, I have argued, was not a conspiracy but rather was a natural way for these deans to think.

Certainly, the Holmes Group members also had intellectual and practical reasons for their proposals. The lesson of my analysis of the political dimension of the proposals is that the intellectual and practical reasons promulgated for the recommendations need to be scrutinized with special care. Is the rationale for these recommendations sound or is it merely a rationalization of political interests?

Notes

1   Alan R. Tom, "A Critique of the Rationale for Extended Teacher Preparation," *Educational Policy*, in press.

2   See Evelyn Di Tosto, "Professional Development Centers: 'The Maryland Approach' " (Baltimore: Maryland State Department of Education, 1976), ERIC Document Reproduction Number: ED 129 808; Gwen P. Yarger and Gerald M. Mager, "Toward Continuous Teacher Education: Collaborative Teaching Centers," *School Organization* 2 (1982): 171-77; and Arthur S. Bolster, Jr., Book review of *The Teaching Hospital: Evolution and Contemporary Issues*, ed. John H. Knowles, *Harvard Educational Review* 37 (Spring 1967): 273-81.

3   Judson T. Shaplin and Henry F. Olds, Jr., eds., *Team Teaching* (New York: Harper & Row, 1964).

4   James B. Conant, *The Education of American Teachers* (New York: McGraw-Hill, 1963).

5   Journalistic accounts of this controversy abound, including Lynn Olson, "Deans' Group Accused of Fostering 'Divisiveness,' " *Education Week*, October 30, 1985, pp. 1, 12; Blake Rodman, "Dissent Emerges within Holmes Group," *Education Week*, January 22, 1986, pp. 1, 10, 16; and Sharon Givens, "Holmes Group Report Gains Praise, but Stirs Dissension," American Association of Colleges for Teacher Education *Briefs* 7 (May-June 1986): 1, 3, 5-6.

6   Carolyn Warner, letter to the editor, *The Chronicle of Higher Education*, May 21, 1986, p. 41.

7   Holmes Group Consortium, *New Standards for Quality in Teacher Education* (East Lansing, Mich.: College of Education, Michigan State University, July 1984), pp. 3, 4.

8   Jean Evangelauf, "Teachers' Colleges Urged to Give Profession Same Status as Law, Medicine," *The Chronicle of Higher Education*, March 12, 1986, pp. 25-26.

9   Givens, "Holmes Group Report," p. 6; Peter J. Quinn, "Eliminating Competition Suspected as Holmes Goal," *Education Week*, April 30, 1986, p. 19; Lynn Olson, "State-College Deans Rap Holmes Report as a 'Source of Conflict,' " *Education Week*, May 7, 1986, p. 7; Association of Independent Liberal Arts Colleges for Teacher Education, "A Call for Dialogue: A Statement concerning the Preparation of Teachers" (The Association: June 4, 1986).

10   Rodman, "Dissent Emerges within Holmes Group," p. 16.

11   Henry W. Holmes, *Shall Teachers Be Scholars*, Occasional Pamphlet No. 1 (Cambridge: Graduate School of Education, Harvard University, 1937), p. 22.

12   Though Instructors do have classroom experience, their ultimate progress toward Professional Teacher status is not presumed by the report. Rather, the Instructor is a temporary teacher who is not expected to devote more than a few years to classroom teaching.

13   Willis D. Hawley, "Toward a Comprehensive Strategy for Addressing the Teacher Shortage," *Phi Delta Kappan* 67 (June 1986): 715-17.

14   Rodman, "Dissent Emerges within Holmes Group," p. 16; and *Teacher Education Reports* 7 (June 6, 1985): 2-3.

Tomorrow's Teachers: Tomorrow's Work

KAREN KEPLER ZUMWALT

Teachers College, Columbia University

Having had the opportunity to read most of the preceding articles in manuscript form and having been a participant in the Holmes Group, Karen Zumwalt is in a position here not only to offer her own reactions to the report as a teacher educator, but also to speak to the general misunderstandings and misgivings that she found voiced in this symposium.

Harry Judge's provocative, impressionistic essay, *American Graduate Schools of Education: A View from Abroad*, took graduate schools of education to task for attempting to mimic graduate schools of arts and sciences rather than becoming true professional schools. He claimed that "by deliberate choice [graduate schools of education] have tended to distance themselves from both the task of training teachers for elementary and secondary schools and that of addressing the problems and needs of those schools."[1] Having been a student or faculty member at three of the schools Judge visited, I found his analysis painfully accurate.[2] That was 1982.

Four years later Judge returned to the United States and, "within hours," he later told me, he knew something had changed. We both agreed that in the intervening years Americans had rediscovered something most educators have always known — the importance of the teacher. In the process, teacher education was once again center stage. Whereas a few years ago few education professors wanted to be called teacher educators, now everyone had ideas about teacher education. Most miraculously, a group of deans, from the very research-intensive universities Judge had chided, had placed teacher education at the top of their agendas. They backed their commitment by accepting the arduous task of collectively developing an agenda for reform. The very existence of *Tomorrow's Teachers*, regardless of the eventual impact of particular recommendations, is cause for celebration.

As one of the non-dean participants in the development of the reform agenda, I have a special appreciation for the courage of the deans and the effort involved in writing a collective report intended to preclude "business as usual." Institutional self-interest, differing conceptions of teacher education, pragmatic considerations, and the inevitable clash of academic egos led to lively dialogue and some frustrating and discouraging times, but the deans persisted. They have provided faculty with a thoughtful, ambitious, challenging agenda as a starting point for a long overdue consideration of teacher education and teaching on our university campuses.

The report holds the promise of sustained attention and resources devoted to teacher education in Holmes Group institutions. For teacher educators, long used to being considered second-class citizens by too many of their faculty colleagues, this indicates exciting times of collaboration in program development and research. The potential opportunity for funded collaborative work with teacher educators from other institutions committed to a similar reform agenda is especially inviting.

Rather than viewing *Tomorrow's Teachers* as a final report, I regard it as a starting point for intra- and interuniversity dialogue and development. The set of reaction papers in this symposium will help facilitate the dialogue by highlighting the many problematic areas that must be addressed in the coming years — differentiated staffing, teacher examinations, changes in schools as work places, teacher certification, undergraduate teacher education programs, teacher supply, issues of equity, professional development schools, the role of administrators, the nature and quality of liberal arts education, the reward structure of the university, the development of professional dispositions, the nature of professional knowledge and conceptions of good teaching.

In the next few years, it is likely that some elements of the reform agenda will evolve differently than presently envisioned; some elements may be dropped, and there may be substantial additions. As some of the reactors suggest, maybe the medical metaphor is inappropriate, maybe the hope of simultaneous change in universities, schools, and state certification procedures is unrealistic, and maybe we will never reach consensus on the actual components of professional education. Or maybe the critics will prove to be overly pessimistic. Remarkably, the deans in the Holmes Group have put aside their usual academic reserve and cautiousness, realizing that the problems probably defy definitive solutions and that unless someone has the courage to propose and pursue change, little will happen.

During the past two years, these deans have demonstrated an understanding that the actual reform as well as the process of reform will be evolving over the next five planning years. They struggled with the level of generality for their recommendations, realizing a need for enough specificity to provide direction and promise of more than superficial change, with enough generality to permit the necessary and desirable faculty and institutional dialogue. For example, while some reactors were frustrated by the general description of the professional education components, more would have been appalled if the group had defined *the* professional curriculum. The deans had to find a balance between general guidelines and specific prescriptions. Having seen more specific and more general drafts, I think they have succeeded remarkably well in the final draft of the report. They clearly take a stance yet they also accept the inevitable evolutionary process and leave considerable room for faculty and institutional discretion. It is an action plan, but discussion and development are built into the plan for the next five years.

The issues and problems raised by the contributors to this symposium offer much to think and talk about. Having been a participant in the development of the reform agenda and having read most of the papers prepared for this special issue, I do feel a need to respond to a few misunderstandings, many of which I have seen elsewhere, as well as to relate some of my own concerns as a teacher educator.

In reading through the symposium papers, I was struck by the fact that almost every aspect of the report was controversial except for the internship year, and that misunderstandings seem to center in the areas "closest to home." Contrary to the views of some reactors, *Tomorrow's Teachers* does not state that all study of education must be at the graduate level nor that all master's work must be at "autonomous graduate schools of education" affiliated with major research universities. Rather, the deans suggest that "a sound study of education, whether at the graduate or undergraduate level, would provide a way of understanding schooling in the same way that the study of any discipline illuminates a set of phenomena. In this sense, education is one of the arts and sciences since it applies tested modes of inquiry to a phenomenon of universal scope and significance" (p. 51). Some institutions might want to offer education courses in a "pre-ed" package, while others may wish to offer courses involving the "social-philosophical context" later in teachers' preparation when they might have more meaning. The deans did state, however, that the professional study of education leading to certification should take place largely at the graduate level, allowing for a more adequate preparation in the liberal arts and subject matter specialty. They were not naive enough to think that research universities would be the only nor even the main site of the preparation of Professional Teachers at the master's level (p. 41). In their vision, colleges might choose to prepare Instructors or Professional Teachers if they could develop masters' programs (which many have already done). Other universities, not identified by the Holmes Group for membership, could choose to prepare all three groups of teachers if they could meet the standards required for the preparation of Career Professional.

The three-tier system of certification was also a source of misunderstanding. A doctorate is *not* stated as a requirement for Career Professionals, and a Career Professional is not just another name for today's administrator. This tier is proposed to give teachers the opportunity to advance without leaving the classroom: "Opportunities for educational leadership must be combined with teaching itself to keep such teachers actively committed to improving their schools" (p. 40). Likewise, Instructor is not just a new name for untenured teachers because they are not eligible for tenure "without at least a year of carefully supervised practice [internship], and advanced study in pedagogy and human learning" (pp. 10–11). Nor is Instructor a new name for substitutes and emergency license teachers. The Instructor tier is an attempt to break the supply-and-demand cycle of unqualified persons serving as regular classroom teachers. It closes the back door into lifetime teaching positions. These Instructors, unlike emergency license teachers, must have a BA in a subject area, pass a written exam in their subject area, pass general tests in reading and writing and a test of "the rudiments of pedagogy" (p. 11). Before being issued an Instructor's certificate and assuming responsibility for a classroom under supervision, they would also have to take several months of full-time study. While not ideal, this tier does less to undermine the profession and is in fact a vast improvement over the present practice of hiring unqualified "Labor Day Specials" who often stay on for years. And unlike the claim of one reactor, the existence of the Instructor tier does break the linear model of academic study, professional study, and internship before practice.

The elementary/secondary distinction also led to some confusion. Nowhere does the Holmes Group take a stand directly or indirectly for departmentalized as opposed to self-contained elementary school classrooms. Although one reactor claims that the Holmes Group proposal differentiates more between elementary and secondary teacher preparation, in actuality, the agenda calls for making their preparation more similar than presently exists by increasing the liberal arts work for elementary teachers and increasing professional education work for secondary teachers.

The authors of *Tomorrow's Teachers* have avoided reducing their proposals to meaningless abstractions for the sake of appeasing all parties. While this decision is to be applauded, it also means that individual participants, while accepting the thrust of the report, will find some aspects of the report troublesome or even wrongheaded. This is to be expected if a group wants to boldly state a position to stimulate interest and dialogue rather than to produce a final, definitive statement acceptable to all. It should also encourage continued dialogue and development rather than an "accept-reject" reaction.

For me, the statement about the "promise of a science of education . . . about to be fulfilled" (p. 52) and others implying an applications view of knowledge not only create unrealistic expectations but cast a technical orientation on teaching that I think undermines efforts to improve teaching and teacher education.[3] Obviously, this concern represents a tension within our own field — a healthy tension that I hope will be addressed but left unresolved in future discussions and in the development of actual reforms. I know, from participating in the group, that there is an acceptance of legitimate differences, which may have been underplayed in the attempt to write a clear, crisp report that captures the attention of the public as well as the usual professional audiences.

Acceptance of diversity of views, however, is bound to lead to some contradictory statements. For instance, the report declares that interactive teaching is the "hallmark of competent professionals" (p. 28). The judgmental aspects of teaching are recognized. Interactive teaching involves deliberations, compromises, and decisions by the teacher before, during, and after teaching. The teacher plans the curriculum ahead of time but the curriculum also evolves as the teacher engages a particular group of students in study. Hence, preparing people to teach is much more complicated than training them with a set of skills that will solve the problems of teaching. As Darling-Hammond comments in this issue, the Holmes Group's vision of good teaching is "its most cogent rationale for its proposals to strengthen teacher education." It is a vision I share and one that also helps me put the troublesome "science of education" comments in context.

This vision of good teaching also makes me uncomfortable with the description of an Instructor whose lessons are planned by someone else. If good teaching is truly interactive, how can having Instructors' "lessons structured and reviewed by professional teachers" (p. 38) be possible or acceptable? This is a vision of the teacher as an implementor of curriculum created by someone else — a vision contrary to the image of interactive teaching promoted elsewhere in the report. The Instructor tier may be desirable and/or necessary, but in theory and in practice it demands much more consideration.

Such concerns and others expressed in this special issue will undoubtedly be addressed because the authors of this report have established a process for further deliberation and development. By creating a process for enlarging and reestablishing the Holmes Group, the authors are trying to avoid having *Tomorrow's Teachers* take its place on the shelf as evidence of another passing interest in teacher education. For those who join the enlarged Holmes Group, the report is far from "self-serving," as some have charged. Joining means a commitment to do things differently. "Self-serving" for these institutions would be to continue the drift away from a professional school model toward an arts and science model at research-intensive universities. Countering this trend, the Holmes Group deans are proposing an ambitious agenda for reform in teaching, in teacher education, *and* at their own institutions. Whether the Holmes Group reform agenda has a long-term impact on teaching and teacher education in this country is yet to be seen, but the mere existence of such a collaboratively written report initiated by a group of deans is noteworthy in itself and belies the common belief that "there will be no reform if we wait for educators to introduce it."[4]

Notes

1   Harry Judge, *American Graduate Schools of Education: A View from Abroad* (New York: Ford Foundation, 1982), p. 6.

2   See Karen Kepler Zumwalt, Review of Harry Judge, *American Graduate Schools of Education: A View from Abroad*, *Teachers College Record* 85, no. 1 (Fall 1983): 150–54.

3   See Karen Kepler Zumwalt, "Research on Teaching: Policy Implications for Teacher Education," in *Policy-Making in Education*, Eighty-first Yearbook of the National Society for the Study of Education, Part I, ed. Ann Lieberman and Milbrey Wallin McLaughlin (Chicago: University of Chicago Press, 1982); and idem, ed., *Improving Teaching*, 1986 Yearbook of the Association of Supervision and Curriculum Development (Alexandria, Va.: ASCD, 1986).

4   Francis Griffith, "Teachers Are Part of the Problem," *The University Bookman*, Autumn 1982, p. 16.

CONTRIBUTORS

PHILIP G. ALTBACH is chair and professor in the department of educational organization, administration, and policy, State University of New York at Buffalo. He is also director of the comparative education center.

MICHAEL W. APPLE is professor of curriculum and instruction and educational policy studies at the University of Wisconsin, Madison. Among his recent volumes are *Ideology and Curriculum* and *Education and Power*. A new work, *Teachers and Texts: A Political Economy of Class and Gender Relations in Education*, has recently been published.

SAMUEL B. BACHARACH is professor of organizational behavior in Cornell University's New York State School of Industrial and Labor Relations. His published work focuses on organizational analysis and design, quality of work life, compensation, and bargaining. Among his books are *Organizational Behavior in Schools and School Districts* and *Power and Politics in Organizations*.

MERLE BORROWMAN is professor of education at the University of California, Berkeley. He has taught the history of education at Teachers College, Columbia University, the University of Wisconsin, and the University of California, Berkeley. He has written two books and many articles on the history of teacher education.

SHARON C. CONLEY is assistant professor of educational administration at the University of Arizona, Tucson, and senior consultant, Organizational Analysis & Practice, Inc., Ithaca, New York. Her research focuses on organizational behavior in schools and school districts, career development, and job design.

LARRY CUBAN is a professor in the administration and policy analysis program at the School of Education, Stanford University. He has served as a superintendent, district office administrator, and high school teacher. He is completing a book on the practice of leadership in public schools.

LINDA DARLING-HAMMOND is a senior social scientist and director of the education and human resources program at the Rand Corporation. Her research focuses on the effects of policies on teachers and teaching practices.

ROBERT DREEBEN is professor in the department of education, University of Chicago. He does research on the social organization of schooling, and is co-author with Rebecca Barr of *How Schools Work*.

WALTER FEINBERG is professor of philosophy of education at the University of Illinois, Urbana-Champaign. His latest books are *Understanding Education* (Cambridge University Press, 1983), and, with Jonas F. Soltis, *School and Society* (Teachers College Press, 1985).

MARY HATWOOD FUTRELL, a business education teacher in Alexandria, Virginia, is the president of the 1.8 million-member National Education Association.

PHILIP W. JACKSON is the David Lee Shillinglaw Distinguished Service Professor in the department of education and behavioral sciences at the University of Chicago. He is also director of the Benton Center for curriculum and instruction.

BRUCE JOYCE is one of the directors of Booksend Laboratories, Eugene, Oregon. He specializes in research on models of teaching, staff development, and school improvement and provides institutes and seminars for school district and higher education personnel who are responsible for the design of training and school improvement programs and initiatives. His recent books include *Schooling Improvement* (Longman), and the third edition of *Models of Teaching* (Prentice Hall).

HARRY JUDGE is director of the Oxford University Department of Educational Studies. His main interests cover the development of secondary education in Great Britain and the reform of teacher education. Recent publications include *American Graduate Schools of Education: A View from Abroad* (1982) and *A Generation of Schooling* (1984).

ANN LIEBERMAN is professor in the area of policy, governance, and administration and executive director of the Puget Sound Educational Consortium, University of Washington. Her position is an attempt to link the College of Education to a group of schools surrounding the Seattle area. She has recently edited *Rethinking School Improvement: Research, Craft, and Concept* (Teachers College Press). She has long been active in working with and writing about professional development and practice.

JANE ROLAND MARTIN is professor of philosophy at the University of Massachusetts, Boston. She is the author of numerous articles on education, and her most recent book is *Reclaiming a Conversation: The Ideal of the Educated Woman* (Yale University Press, 1985).

MARY ANNE RAYWID is professor of education at Hofstra University where she also chairs the department of administration and policy studies. Her current research includes schools of choice and other contemporary reform proposals.

KEVIN RYAN is professor of education at Boston University. He has taught on the faculties of Stanford University, the University of Chicago, Harvard University and The Ohio State University. Currently, he is director of the Character Education Project.

MICHAEL W. SEDLAK is associate professor at Michigan State University and a senior researcher with the Institute for Research on Teaching. He has published widely in the history of education, professional schooling, and youth policy. His most recent book is *Selling Students Short: Classroom Bargains and Academic Reform in the American High School* (New York: Teachers College Press, 1986).

ALBERT SHANKER has been president of the American Federation of Teachers since 1974 and was president of New York City's United Federation of Teachers from 1964 until his retirement last year. He has published widely and was recently elected to the National Academy of Education.

ALAN R. TOM is professor and chairman of the department of education at Washington University, St. Louis. He was one of the members who planned the Holmes agenda and is completing his term as president of the Association of Independent Liberal Arts Colleges for Teacher Education. Tom has published on such topics as program accreditation and the relationship of educational research and practice.

KAREN KEPLER ZUMWALT, associate professor of education and chair of the department of curriculum and teaching at Teachers College, Columbia University, was a member of the writing and coordinating committee of the Holmes Group. As a faculty resource person, she brought her experience as a teacher educator at a liberal arts college (Smith) and at Teachers College, where she directed the preservice program in elementary education. She is currently conducting a study of teacher education reforms in New Jersey, with Gary Natriello, under the auspices of the National Center for Research on Teacher Education. Her most recent publication is the 1986 ASCD Yearbook, *Improving Teaching*.

INDEX

JUL 22 1988

LIBRARY
OF
MOUNT ST. MARY'S
COLLEGE
EMMITSBURG, MARYLAND